Footprint Handbook
Angkor
ANDREW SPOONER

This is
Angkor

A vast and elaborately detailed complex, the ancient temple city of Angkor Wat has remained the heart and soul of Cambodia for almost two millennia. And, despite the ever-growing throngs of visitors, this historical site still exceeds expectation. Included in the gargantuan complex lie legions of magical temples which attest to the ability of bygone artisans. Visitors also flock to jungle-clad Ta Prohm, where tenatacle-like foliage entwined around the temple provides an insight into how earlier explorers would have discovered it.

The town of Siem Reap has graduated from Angkor's service centre to an international tourist hub, teeming with modern restaurants and upmarket hotels. Fortunately the settlement still retains much if its original charm. A short trip from Siem Reap is the Tonlé Sap, Southeast Asia's largest freshwater lake, scattered with many floating villages.

Andrew Spooner

Best of
Angkor

❶ Angkor Wat

The biggest religious monument in the world, Angkor Wat, the ancient capital of the powerful Khmer Empire, is the spiritual and cultural heart of Cambodia. The vast 12th-century complex is considered the prime example of Classical Khmer art and architecture. Visit at sunrise for the most memorable views. Page 14.

❷ Angkor Thom

The royal city of Angkor Thom, with its 100-m-wide moat once probably stocked with crocodiles to deter the enemy, is 4 km from Angkor Wat. At its geometric centre is the imposing Bayon temple whose large beaming faces have now become synonymous with the Angkor complex. Pages 18 and 22.

3 Ta Prohm

For all would-be Mouhots and closet Indiana Joneses, the temple of Ta Prohm is the perfect lost-in-the-jungle experience. Built to house the divine image of the Queen Mother, it has only been minimally cleared of undergrowth, fig trees and creepers and is widely regarded as one of Angkor's most enchanting and beautiful temples. Page 29.

• 5

❹ Banteay Srei

North of Angkor and 25 km from Ta Prohm, Banteay Srei, meaning 'Citadel of Women', is a much smaller temple, noted for the quality of its craftsmanship and considered by many historians to be the highest achievement of art from the Angkor period. Page 40.

❺ Tonlé Sap

The largest freshwater lake in Southeast Asia, the Tonlé Sap is of major importance to Cambodia and is home to many ethnic Vietnamese and numerous Cham communities, who live in floating villages around the lake. Uniquely, the Tonlé Sap River, a tributary of the Mekong, reverses its flow and runs uphill for six months of the year. Page 44.

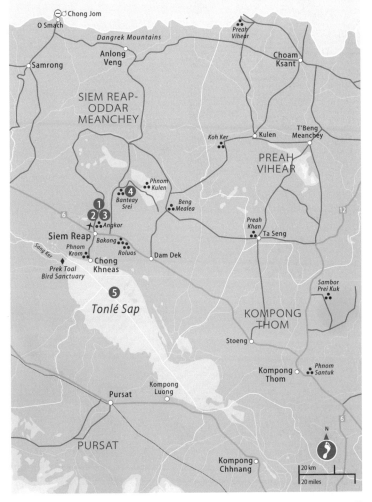

THAILAND

Chong Jom
O Smach
Dangrek Mountains
Preah
Vihear
Anlong
Veng
Choam
Ksant
Samrong
SIEM REAP-
ODDAR
MEANCHEY
Koh Ker
Kulen
T'Beng
Meanchey
Phnom
Kulen
PREAH
VIHEAR
④
Banteay
Srei
Beng
Mealea
①
②③
Angkor
Siem Reap
Bakong
Preah
Khan
Phnom
Krom
Roluos
Ta Seng
Sang Ker
Chong
Khneas
Dam Dek
Prek Toal
Bird Sanctuary
⑤
Tonlé Sap
Sambor
Prei Kuk
KOMPONG
THOM
Stoeng
Kompong
Thom
Phnom
Santuk
Pursat
Kompong
Luong
PURSAT
Kompong
Chhnang

N

20 km
20 miles

Sights
Angkor

The huge temple complex of Angkor, the ancient capital of the powerful Khmer Empire, is one of the archaeological treasures of Asia and the spiritual and cultural heart of Cambodia. Angkor Wat is arguably the greatest temple within the complex, both in terms of grandeur and sheer magnitude. After all, it is the biggest religious monument in the world, its outer walls clad with one of the longest continuous bas-relief ever created. The diverse architectural prowess and dexterity of thousands of artisans is testified by around 100 brilliant monuments in the area. Of these, the Bayon (with its beaming smiles), Banteay Srei (which features the finest intricate carvings) and the jungle temple of Ta Prohm are unmissable. However, some people prefer the understated but equally brilliant temples of Neak Pean, Preah Khan and Pre Rup.

Essential How to do Angkor

Getting around

Angkor Thom is in the centre of the temple complex, about 4 km away from Angkor Wat and Preah Khan. One road connects the temples. Most of the temples within the Angkor complex (except the Roluos Group) are located in an area 8 km north of Siem Reap, with the area extending across a 25-km radius. The Roluos Group is 13 km east of Siem Reap and further away is Banteay Srei (32 km).

Snapshot

Cambodia Angkor Air offers several daily flights between Siem Reap and Phnom Penh. (There are also now thrice-weekly flights to/from Sihanoukville.) From July-March daily **river ferries** ply the Tonlé Sap river and lake between Phnom Penh and Siem Reap.

Bicycle Bicycle hire, US$2-3 per day from most guesthouses, represents a nice option for those who feel reasonably familiar with the area. The **White Bicycles** scheme, www. thewhitebicycles.org, set up by Norwegian expats, offers bikes for US$2 per day with US$1.50 of that going straight into local charities and no commission to the hotels. If you only have a day or two to explore you won't be able to cover many of the temples on a pedal bike due to the searing temperatures and sprawling layout. Angkor Wat and Banteay Srei have official bicycle parking sites (1000 riel) and at the other temples you can quite safely park and lock your bikes in front of a drink stall.

Car with driver and guide These are available from larger hotels for US$25-30 per day plus US$25 for a guide. An excellent service is provided by **Mr Hak**, T012-540336, www. angkortaxidriver.com, who offers packages and tours around Angkor and the surrounding area. The **Angkor Tour Guide Association** and most other travel agencies can also organize this.

Elephant These are stationed near the Bayon or at the South Gate of Angkor Thom during the day. In the evenings, they are located at the bottom of Phnom Bakheng, taking tourists up to the summit for sunset.

Helicopter You can also charter a helicopter, see page 54.

Moto Expect to pay US$10-12 per day for a moto unless the driver speaks good English, in which case the price will be higher. This price will cover trips to the Roluos Group of temples but not to Banteay Srei. No need to add more than a dollar or two to the price for getting to Banteay Srei unless the driver is also a guide and can demonstrate that he is genuinely going to show you around.

Tuk-tuk have appeared in recent years and a trip to the temples on a motorbike-drawn cart is a popular option for two people, U$14-17 a day.

Guides

Guides can be invaluable when navigating the temples. Most hotels and travel agents will be able to point you in the direction of a good guide. The **Khmer Angkor Tour Guide Association**, on the road to Angkor, T063-964347, www.khmerangkortourguide.com, has well-trained and well-briefed guides; some speak English better than others. The going rate is US$20-25 per day.

Temple fees and hours

The **Angkor Pass** can only be bought at official ticket booths, which are on the road from Siem Reap to Angkor Wat. The checkpoint on the road from the airport to Angkor Wat and the checkpoint at Banteay Srei also have one-day Angkor Passes, but not three-day and seven-day passes.

A **one-day** pass costs US$20, three-day pass US$40, **seven-day** pass US$60 (free for children under 12) and must be paid in cash (US dollars, Cambodian riel, Thai baht or euro accepted). Passes for **three** and **seven days** are issued with a photograph, which is taken on location. The seven-day pass is valid for any seven days (they don't have to be consecutive) one month from the purchase date. Most people will be able to cover the majority of the temples within three days. If you buy your ticket after 1715 the day before, you get a free sunset thrown in. The complex is open daily 0500-1800.

You will need to pay additional fees if you wish to visit Beng Melea (US$5), Phnom Kulen (US$20) or Koh Ker (US$10); payable at the individual sites.

Beating the crowds

Avoiding traffic within the Angkor complex is difficult but achievable. If you reverse the order of the standard tours, peak hour traffic at major temples is dramatically reduced. As many tour groups troop into Siem Reap for lunch this is an opportune time to catch a peaceful moment in the complex, just bring a packed lunch.

Security

Landmines planted on some outlying paths have nearly all been cleared, but it is still safer to stick to well-used paths. Be wary of snakes in the dry season. The very poisonours Hanuman snake (lurid green) is fairly common in the area.

To avoid the masses at the draw-card attraction, Angkor Wat, try to walk around the temple, as opposed to through it. Sunset at Phnom Bakheng has turned into a circus fiasco, so aim for Angkor or the Bayon at this time as they are both quiet in comparison.

Sunrise is still relatively peaceful at Angkor, grab yourself the prime position behind the left-hand pond (you need to depart Siem Reap no later than 0530), though there are other stunning early morning options, such as Srah Srang or Bakong. Bakheng gives a beautiful vista of Angkor in the early-mid morning.

When to go

November-February (the driest and coolest time of year, which can still be unbearably hot). This is the peak visitor season and so can be crowded. The monsoon is from June to October/November. At this time it can get very muddy but it's a great time to photograph the temples as the foliage is lush and there is less dust. April can be furnace-like and unpleasantly dusty.

Tip...

Everybody wants to visit Angkor Wat and Angkor Thom, but do visit Ta Prohm, which has been left in an unrestored state; you will certainly get the atmosphere, especially if you go late afternoon.

How much time to allow?

The temples are scattered over an area in excess of 160 sq km. There are three so-called 'circuits'. The **Petit Circuit** takes in the main central temples including Angkor Wat, Bayon, Baphuon and the Terrace of the Elephants. The **Grand Circuit** takes a wider route, including smaller temples like Ta Prohm, East

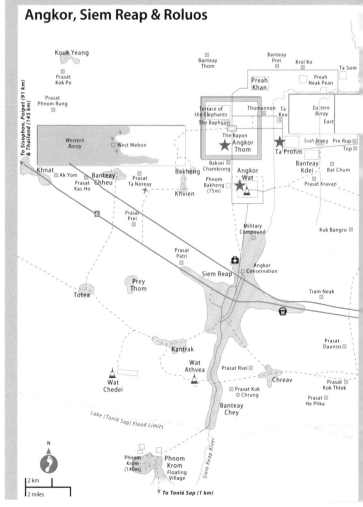

Angkor, Siem Reap & Roluos

Mebon and Neak Pean. The **Roluos Group Circuit** ventures further afield still, taking in the temples near Roluos: Lolei, Preah Ko and Bakong. Here are some options for visiting Angkor's temples:

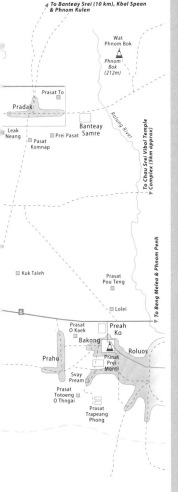

To Banteay Srei (10 km), Kbal Spean & Phnom Kulen

Wat Phnom Bok

Phnom Bok (212m)

Prasat To

Pradak

Leak Neang Prei Pasat Banteay Samre

Pasat Komnap

Roluing River

To Chau Srei Vibol Temple Complex (5km approx)

Kuk Taleh

Prasat Pou Teng

To Beng Melea & Phnom Penh

Lolei

Prasat O Kaek   Preah Ko

Bakong

Prahu

Roluos

Prasat Prei Monti

Svay Pream

Prasat Totoeng O Thngai

Prasat Trapeang Phong

Half day
South Gate of Angkor Thom, Bayon, Angkor Wat.

One day
Angkor Wat (sunrise or sunset), South Gate of Angkor Thom, Angkor Thom Complex (Bayon, Elephant Terrace, Royal Palace) and Ta Prohm. This is a hefty schedule for one day; you'll need to arrive after 1615 and finish just after 1700 the following day.

Two days
The same as above but with the inclusion of the rest of the Angkor Thom, Preah Khan, Srah Srang (sunrise) and, at a push, Banteay Srei.

Three days
Day 1 Sunrise at Angkor Wat; morning South Gate of Angkor Thom, Angkor Thom complex (aside from Bayon); Ta Prohm; late afternoon-sunset at the Bayon.

Day 2 Sunrise Srah Srang; morning Banteay Kdei and Banteay Srei; late afternoon Preah Khan; sunset at Angkor Wat.

Day 3 Sunrise and morning Roluos; afternoon Ta Keo and sunset either at Bakheng or Angkor Wat.

Those choosing to stay one or two days longer should try to work Banteay Samre, East Mebon, Neak Pean and Thomannon into their itinerary. A further two to three days warrants a trip to Prasat Kravan, Ta Som, Beng Melea and Kbal Spean.

★ The awe-inspiring sight of Angkor Wat first thing in the morning is something you're not likely to forget. Constructed between 1113 and 1150, it is believed to be the biggest religious monument ever built and certainly one of the most spectacular. British historian Arnold Toynbee said in his book *East to West* that: "Angkor is not orchestral; it is monumental." That sums it up. The temple complex covers 81 ha and is comparable in size to the Imperial Palace in Beijing. Its five towers are emblazoned on the Cambodian flag and the 12th-century masterpiece is considered by art historians to be the prime example of Classical Khmer art and architecture. It took more than 30 years to build and is contemporary with Nôtre-Dame in Paris and Durham Cathedral in England. The temple is dedicated to the Hindu god Vishnu, personified in earthly form by its builder, the god-king Suryavarman II, and is aligned east to west.

Construction and orientation

Angkor Wat differs from other temples primarily because it is facing westward, symbolically the direction of death, leading many to believe it was a tomb. However, as Vishnu is associated with the west, it is now generally accepted that it served both as a temple and a mausoleum for the king. The sandstone was probably quarried from a far-away mine and floated down the Siem Reap river on rafts. Like other Khmer temple mountains, Angkor Wat is an architectural allegory, depicting in stone the epic tales of Hindu mythology. The central sanctuary of the temple complex represents the sacred Mount Meru, the centre of the Hindu universe, on whose summit the gods reside. Angkor Wat's five towers symbolize Meru's five peaks; the enclosing wall represents the mountains at the edge of the world and the surrounding moat, the ocean beyond.

Angkor Wat was found in much better condition than most of the other temples in the complex because it seems to have been continuously inhabited by Buddhist monks after the Thais invaded in 1431. They were able to keep back the encroaching jungle. A giant stone Buddha was placed in the hall of the highest central tower, formerly sacred to the Hindu god, Vishnu. Three modern Buddhist monasteries flank the wat.

The complex

The temple complex is enclosed by a **square moat** – more than 5 km long and 190 m wide – and a high, galleried wall, which is covered in epic bas-reliefs and has four ceremonial tower gateways. The main gateway faces west and the temple is approached by a 475-m-long road, built along a **causeway**, which is lined with **naga balustrades**. There are small rectangular barays on either side of the roadway. To either side of the balustrades are two isolated buildings, thought to have been **libraries** – there are two more pairs of them within the temple precincts on the first and second terraces.

At the far end of the causeway stands a **cruciform platform**, guarded by stone lions, from which the devaraja may have held audiences; his backdrop being the three-tiered central sanctuary. Commonly referred to as the **Terrace of Honour**, it is entered through the colonnaded processional gateway of the outer gallery. The transitional enclosure beyond it is again cruciform in shape. Its four quadrants formed galleries, once stocked full of statues of the Buddha. Only a handful of the original 1000-odd images remain. Each gallery also had a basin which would originally have contained water for priests' ritual ablution. The second terrace, which is also square, rises from behind the **Gallery of a Thousand Buddhas**. It has a tower at each corner.

The cluster of **central towers**, 12 m above the second terrace, is reached by 12 steep stairways which represent the precipitous slopes of Mount Meru. Many historians believe that the upwards hike to this terrace was reserved for the high priests and king himself. Today, anyone is welcome but the difficult climb is best handled slowly by stepping sideways up the steep incline. The five lotus flower-shaped sandstone towers – the first appearance of these features in Khmer architecture – are believed to have once been covered in gold. The eight-storey towers are square, although they appear octagonal, and give the impression of a sprouting bud. Above the ascending tiers of roofs – each jutting gable has an elaborately carved pediment – the tower tapers into a circular roof. A quincunx shape is formed by the towers with four on each corner and another marking the centre. The central tower is dominant, and is the Siva shrine and principal sanctuary, whose pinnacle rises more than 30 m above the third level and 55 m above ground level. This sanctuary would have contained an image of Siva in the likeness of King Suryavarman II, as it was his temple-mountain. But it is now a Buddhist shrine and contains statues of the Buddha. The steps leading up to the third level are worn and very steep. On the south side the steps have a hand rail (not recommended for vertigo sufferers).

Bas-reliefs

Over 1000 sq m of bas-relief decorate the temple. Its greatest sculptural treasure is the 2-m-high bas-relief, around the walls of the outer gallery. It is the longest continuous bas-relief in the world. In some areas traces of the paint and gilt that once covered the carvings can still be seen. Most famous are the hundreds of figures of devatas and apsaras in niches along the walls. The apsaras – the celestial women – are modelled on the god-king's own bevy of bare-breasted beauties and the sculptors' attention to detail provides an insight into the world of 12th-century haute couture. Their hair is often knotted on the crown and bejewelled – although all manner of wild and exotic coiffures are depicted. Jewelled collars and hip-girdles also are common and bracelets worn on the upper arms. Sadly many of the apsaras have been removed in recent years.

The bas-reliefs narrate stories from the *Ramayana* and *Mahabharata*, as well as legends of Vishnu, and are reminiscent of Pallava and Chola art in southeast India. Pious artisans and peasants were probably only allowed as far as Angkor Wat's outer gallery, where they could admire the bas-reliefs and pay homage to the god-king. In the open courtyards, statues of animals enliven the walls. Lions stand on guard beside the staircases. There were supposed to be 300 of them in the original

ANGKOR WAT

Anti-clockwise round the bas-reliefs

❶ West gallery, southern half represents a scene from the Hindu *Mahabharata* epic. The Battle of Kurukshtra shows the clash between the Pandavas (with pointed headdresses, attacking from the right) and the Kauravas. The two armies come from the two ends of the panel and meet in the middle in a ferocious battle. Above the war scene is Bhima, head of the Kauravas, wounded and lying atop a pile of arrows, surrounded by grieving followers and loved ones. The centre of the sculpture reveals the chief of the Pandavas in his war chariot. (The larger the figure the more important the person.) The southwest corner has been badly damaged – some say by the Khmer Rouge – but shows scenes from Vishnu's life.

❷ South gallery, western half depicts Suryavarman II (builder of Angkor Wat) leading a procession. He is riding a royal elephant and carrying an axe, giving orders to his army before leading them into battle against the Chams. Shade is provided to him by 15 umbrellas, while a gamut of servants cool him with fans. The rank of the army officers is indicated by the number of umbrellas. Other troops follow on elephants. While trailing behind them are musicians and priests bearing holy fire. The undisciplined, outlandishly dressed figures are the Thais helping the Khmers in battle against the Chams.

❸ South gallery, eastern half was restored in 1946. It depicts the punishments and rewards one can expect in the afterlife. On the left-hand side, the upper and middle levels show the dead waiting for their moment of judgement with Yama (Judge of the Dead) and his assistants, Dharma and Sitragupta, as to whether they will go to either the 37 heavens or 32 hells. On the left, lead two roads one to the heavens (above), and the other to hell (below). The damned, depicted in the bottom row, are in for a rough ride: the chances of their being savaged by wild animals, seized by demons or having their tongues pulled out (or any combination thereof) are quite high. Yama was tough and some might suggest that the crime didn't exactly fit the punishment: those who damaged others' property received broken bones; gluttons were sawn in half, and those who picked Shiva's flowers had their heads nailed. The blessed, depicted in the upper two rows, are borne along in palanquins surrounded by large numbers of bare-breasted apsaras dancing on lotuses.

❹ Eastern gallery, southern half is a 50-m-long panel that's probably Angkor's best known. The Churning of the Sea of Milk, portrays part of the Hindu legend, Bhagavata-Pourana. On the North are 92 deva (gods) and on the South 88 asura (demons) battling to win the coveted ambrosia (the nectar of the gods which gives immortality).

The serpent, Vasuki, is caught, quite literally, in the centre of their dispute. The asura hold onto the head of the serpent, whilst the devas hold the tail. The fighting causes the waters to churn, which in turn produces the elixir. In the centre, Vishnu commands. Below are sea animals (cut in half by the churning close to the pivot) and above, apsaras encouraging the competitors in their fight for the mighty elixir. Eventually (approximately 1000 years later) the elixir is won by the asuras until Vishnu appears to claim the cup.

⑤ **Eastern gallery, northern half** is unfinished and depicts the garuda-riding Krishna (Vishnu's incarnation) claimong victory over Bana for the possession of the ambrosia. The gate in the centre of the east gallery was used by Khmer royalty and dignitaries for mounting and dismounting elephants.

⑥ **North gallery, eastern half** shows Garuda-riding, Krishna claiming victory over the demons. Most of the other scenes are from the *Ramayana*, notably the visit of Hanuman (the monkey god) to Sita.

⑦ **North gallery, western half** pictures another battle scene: demons versus gods. Twenty-one gods are pictured including Varuna, god of water, standing on a five-headed naga; Skanda, the god of war (several heads and a peacock with arms); Yama, the god of dead (chariot drawn by oxen): and Suva, the sun god (standing on a disc).

⑧ **Western gallery, northern half** has another scene from the *Ramayana* depicting another battle between the devas and asuras – this time in the form of Rama and Ravana. The demon king Ravana, who rides on a chariot pulled by monsters and commands an army of giants, has seduced and abducted Rama's beautiful wife Sita. The battle takes place in the centre of the relief.

Angkor Wat

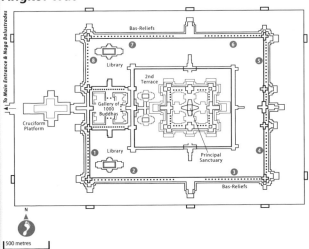

building. Part of the bas-reliefs were hit by shrapnel in 1972, and some of its apsaras were used for target practice.

Temple surrounds

One of the great delights of Angkor, particularly at Angkor Wat, are the glorious trees. Huge tropical trees grow in Angkor's forests – a reminder of how much of Cambodia used to look. Driving out to Angkor from Siem Reap, the flat landscape is largely bare of trees but inside the protected area forests flourish. High in the treetops birds sing and call to each other all day. The wildlife, whose motto seems to be 'always watching: always waiting', is an integral part of Angkor. Keeping the prising tentacles and smothering creepers at bay requires constant vigilance and a sharp blade. A great deal of archaeology is still concealed in the embrace of the forest and exploring the less beaten paths often reveals some unknown and unmapped ruin.

Royal city of Angkor Thom
the empire's massive administrative centre contains the imposing Bayon

Construction

Construction of Jayavarman VII's spacious walled capital, Angkor Thom (which means 'great city'), began at the end of the 12th century: he rebuilt the capital after it had been captured and destroyed by the Cham. Angkor Thom was colossal – the 100-m-wide moat surrounding the city, which was probably stocked with crocodiles as a protection against the enemy, extended more than 12 km. Inside the moat was an 8-m-high stone wall, buttressed on the inner side by a high mound of earth along the top of which ran a terrace for troops to man the ramparts.

The area within the walls was more spacious than that of any walled city in medieval Europe – it could easily have encompassed the whole of ancient Rome. Yet it is believed that this enclosure, like the Forbidden City in Beijing, was only a royal, religious and administrative centre accommodating the court and dignitaries. The rest of the population lived outside the walls between the two artificial lakes – the east and west barays – and along the Siem Reap River.

Four great gateways in the city wall face north, south, east and west and lead to the city's geometric centre, the Bayon. The fifth, Victory Gate, leads from the royal palace (within the Royal Enclosure) to the East Baray. The height of the gates was determined by the headroom needed to accommodate an elephant and howdah complete with parasols. The flanks of each gateway are decorated by three-headed stone elephants and each gateway tower has four giant faces, which keep an eye on all four cardinal points.

Five causeways traverse the moat, each bordered by sculptured balustrades of nagas gripped, on one side, by 54 stern-looking giant gods and on the other by 54 fierce-faced demons. The balustrade depicts the Hindu legend of the churning of the sea (see box, page 19).

Some stone buildings survived the sacking of the city by the Cham, such as the temples of Phimeanakas and Baphuon, and these were incorporated by

ANGKOR THOM

The Churning of the Sea

The Hindu legend, the *Churning of the Sea*, relates how the gods and demons resolved matters in the turbulent days when the world was being created. The elixir of immortality was one of 13 precious things lost in the churning of the cosmic sea. It took 1000 years before the gods and demons, in a joint dredging operation – aided by Sesha, the sea snake, and Vishnu – recovered them all.

The design of the temples of Angkor was based on this ancient legend. The moat represents the ocean and the gods use the top of Mount Meru – represented by the tower – as their churning stick. The cosmic serpent offered himself as a rope to enable the gods and demons to twirl the stick.

Paul Mus, a French archaeologist, suggests that the bridge with the naga balustrades, which went over the moat from the world of men to the royal city, was an image of the rainbow. Throughout Southeast Asia and India, the rainbow is alluded to as a multi-coloured serpent rearing its head in the sky.

Jayavarman in his new plan. He adopted the general layout of the royal centre conceived by Suryavarman II.

Inside Angkor Thom

The **South Gate** provides the most common access route to Angkor Thom, predominantly because it sits on the path between the two great Angkor complexes. The gate is a wonderful introduction to Angkor Thom with well-restored statues of asuras (demons) and gods lining the bridge. The figures on the left, exhibiting serene expression, are the gods, while those on the right, with grimaced, fierce-looking heads, are the asuras. The significance of the naga balustrade, across the moat, is believed to be symbolic of a link between the world of mortals, outside the complex, to the world of gods, inside the complex. The 23-m-high gates feature four faces in a similarly styled fashion to those of the Bayon.

Angkor Thom & around

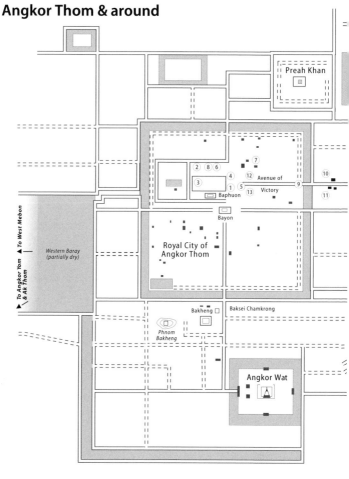

Preah Khan

Avenue of Victory

Baphuon

Bayon

Royal City of Angkor Thom

Western Baray (partially dry)

To West Mebon
To Angkor Yom & Ak Thom

Bakheng

Baksei Chamkrong

Phnom Bakheng

Angkor Wat

N

800 metres
800 yards

Terrace of the Elephants **1**
Royal Enclosure **2**
Phimeanakas **3**
Terrace of the Leper King **4**
Prasats Suor Prat **5**

Tep Tranam **6**
Preah Pithu Group **7**
Preah Palilay **8**
Victory Gate **9**
Thommanon **10**

Chau Say Tevoda **11**
North Kleang **12**
South Kleang **13**

Artificial lakes

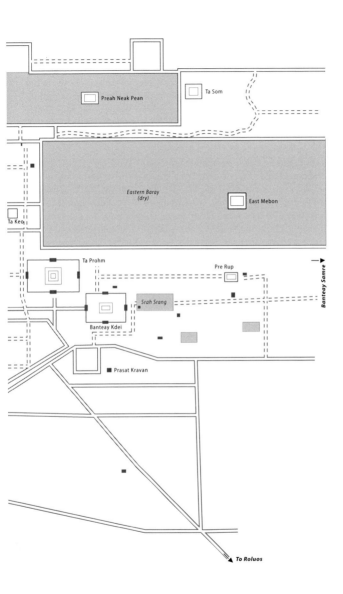

Preah Neak Pean

Ta Som

Eastern Baray (dry)

East Mebon

Ta Keo

Ta Prohm

Pre Rup

Srah Srang

Banteay Kdei

Banteay Samre ►

■ Prasat Kravan

➤ *To Roluos*

★The Bayon

The Bayon is one of Angkor's most famous sights and most people visiting Cambodia are familiar with the beaming faces before even stepping foot in the temple. The Bayon was Jayavarman VII's own temple-mountain, built right in the middle of Angkor Thom; its large faces have now become synonymous with the Angkor complex. It is believed to have been built between the late 12th century to early 13th century, around 100 years after Angkor Wat. Unlike other Khmer monuments, the Bayon has no protective wall immediately enclosing it. The central tower, at the intersection of the diagonals city walls, indicates that the city walls and the temple were built at the same time.

The Bayon is a three-tiered, pyramid temple with a 45-m-high tower, topped by four gigantic carved heads. These faces are believed to be the images of Jayavarman VII as a Bodhisattra, and face the four compass points. They are crowned with lotus flowers, symbol of enlightenment, and are surrounded by 51 smaller towers each with heads facing north, south, east and west. There are over 2000 large faces carved throughout the structure. Although the Bayon seems a complex, labyrinthine structure, its overall layout is quite basic. The first two of the three levels feature galleries of bas-relief (which should be viewed clockwise); a circular central sanctuary dominates the third level.

When Pierre Loti, the French writer, first saw these towers in 1912 he was astounded: "I looked up at the tree-covered towers which dwarfed me, when all of a sudden my blood curdled as I saw an enormous smile looking down on me, and then another smile on another wall, then three, then five, then 10, appearing in every direction". The facial features are striking and the full lips, curling upwards at the corners, are known as 'the smile of Angkor'.

Even the archaeologists of the École Française d'Extrême Orient were not able to decide immediately whether the heads on the Bayon represented Brahma, Siva or the Buddha. There are many theories. One of the most plausible was conceived in 1934 by George Coedès, an archaeologist who spent years studying the temples at Angkor. He postulated that the sculptures represented King Jayavarman VII in the form of Avaloketsvara, the Universal Buddha, implying that the Hindu concept of the god-king had been appended to Buddhist cosmology. Jayavarman VII, once a humble monk who twice renounced the throne and then became the mightiest of all the Khmer rulers, may be the smiling face, cast in stone, at the centre of his kingdom. The multiplication of faces, all looking out to the four cardinal points, may symbolize Jayavarman blessing the four quarters of the kingdom. After Jayavarman's death, the Brahmin priests turned the Bayon into a place of Hindu worship.

The Bayon has undergone a series of facelifts through its life, a point first observed in 1924 by Henri Parmentier – a French archaeologist who worked for L'École Française d'Extrême Orient – and later excavations revealed vestiges of a former building. It is thought that the first temple was planned as a two-tiered structure dedicated to Siva, which was then altered to its present form. As a result, it gives the impression of crowding – the towers rise right next to each other and the courtyards are narrow without much air or light. When Henri Mouhot rediscovered Angkor, local villagers had dubbed the Bayon 'the hide and seek sanctuary' because of its labyrinthine layout.

Bayon bas-reliefs

The bas-reliefs which decorate the walls of the Bayon all seem to tell a story but are much less imposing than those at Angkor Wat. The sculpture is carved deeper but is more naive and less sophisticated than the bas-reliefs at Angkor Wat. They vary greatly in quality, which may have been because the sculptors' skills were being overstretched by Jayavarman's ambitious building programme. The reliefs on the outer wall and on the inner gallery differ completely and seem to belong to two different worlds. The relief on the outside depicts historical events; those on the inside are drawn from the epic world of Hindu gods and legends, representing the creatures who were supposed to haunt the subterranean depths of Mount Meru. In fact the reliefs on the outer wall illustrating historical scenes and derring-do with marauding Cham were carved in the early 13th century during the reign of Jayavarman; those on the inside were carved after the king's death when his successors turned from Mahayana Buddhism back to Hinduism. In total, there are over 1.2 km of bas-reliefs, depicting over 11,000 characters.

Two recurring themes in the bas-reliefs are the powerful king and the Hindu epics. Jayavarman is depicted in the throes of battle with the Cham – who are recognizable thanks to their unusual and distinctive headdress, which looks like an inverted lotus flower. The naval battle pictured on the walls of Banteay Chhmar are almost identical. Funnily enough, there's a bas-relief in the north section of the west gallery depicting a huge fish eating a deer, a complimentary

The Bayon

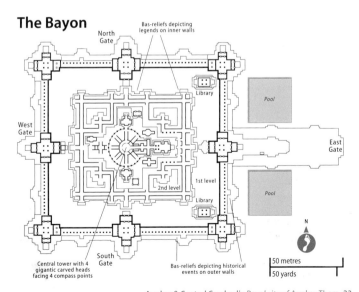

Bas-reliefs depicting legends on inner walls

North Gate

Library

West Gate

Pool

East Gate

1st level

2nd level

Library

Pool

N

Central tower with 4 gigantic carved heads facing 4 compass points

South Gate

Bas-reliefs depicting historical events on outer walls

50 metres
50 yards

ANGKOR

A Chinese emissary's account of his stay at Angkor

One of the most interesting documents relating to the great empire of Angkor is the Chinese emissary Chou Ta-kuan's account of his stay there entitled *Notes on the customs of Cambodia*. The book, written shortly after he had returned to China from a sojourn at Angkor between 1296 and 1297, describes the last days of the kingdom and his role as companion to the Chinese ambassador.

The book is divided into 40 short 'chapters' dealing with aspects of everyday and royal life ranging from childbirth, to justice, to clothing. The account also details aspects of the natural environment (fish and reptiles, birds), the economy of the empire (agriculture, trade, products), and technology (utensils, boats and oars). What makes the account so useful and unusual is that it describes not just the concerns and actions of great men and women, but of everyday life too. The extracts below are just a sample of the insights into everyday Cambodian life during the waning days of the Angkorian Empire. For those intending to visit the site of Angkor, the book (Bangkok: Siam Society, 1993) is highly recommended. It brings to life the ruins of a city, helping you to imagine the place – now so empty – full of people and life.

Cambodian dwellings Out of the [royal] palace rises a golden tower, to the top of which the ruler ascends nightly to sleep. It is common belief that in the tower dwells a genie, formed like a serpent with nine heads, which is Lord of the entire kingdom. Every night this genie appears in the shape of a woman, with whom the sovereign couples. Not even the wives of the king may enter here. At the second watch the king comes forth and is then free to sleep with his wives and his concubines. Should the genie fail to appear for a single night, it is a sign that the king's death is at hand.

Straw thatch covers the dwellings of the commoners, not one of whom would dare place the smallest bit of tile on his roof.

Clothing Every man or woman, from the sovereign down, knots the hair and leaves the shoulders bare. Round the waist they wear a small strip of cloth, over which a large piece is drawn when they leave their houses. Many rules, based on rank, govern the choice of materials. Only the ruler may wear fabrics woven in an all-over pattern.

Women Generally speaking, the women, like the men, wear only a strip of cloth, bound round the waist, showing bare breasts of milky whiteness. As for the concubines and palace girls, I have heard it said that there are from three to five thousand of these, separated into various categories. When a beautiful girl is born into a family, no time is lost in sending her to the palace.

Childbirth Once a Cambodian woman's child is born, she immediately makes a poultice of hot rice and salt and applies it to her private parts. This is taken off in 24 hours, thus preventing any untoward after-effects and causing an astringency which seems to renew the young mother's virginity. When told of this for the first time, my credulity was sorely taxed. However, in the house where I lodged a girl gave birth to a child, and I was able to observe beyond peradventure that the next day she was up carrying the baby in her arms and going with him to bathe in the river. This seems truly amazing!

Everyone with whom I talked said that the Cambodian women are highly sexed. One or two days after giving birth they are ready for intercourse: if a husband is not responsive he will be discarded. When a man is called away on matters of business, they endure his absence for a while; but if he is gone as much as 10 days, the wife is apt to say, "I am no ghost; how can I be expected to sleep alone?"

Slaves Wild men from the hills can be bought to serve as slaves. Families of wealth may own more than 100; those of lesser means content themselves with 10 or 20; only the very poor have none. If a slave should run away and be captured, a blue mark would be tattooed on his face; moreover, an iron collar would be fitted to his neck, or shackles to his arms or legs.

Cambodian justice Points of dispute between citizens, however trifling, are taken to the ruler. In dealing with cases of great seriousness, recourse is not had to strangulation or beheading; outside the West Gate, however, a ditch is dug into which the criminal is placed, earth and stones are thrown back and heaped high, and all is over. Lesser crimes are dealt with by cutting off feet or hands, or by amputation of the nose.

When a thief is caught red-handed, he may be imprisoned and tortured. Recourse is also had to another curious procedure. If an object is missing, and accusation brought against someone who denies the charge, oil is brought to boil in a kettle and the suspected person forced to plunge his hand into it. If he is truly guilty, the hand is cooked to shreds; if not, skin and bones are unharmed. Such is the amazing way of these barbarians.

Products of Cambodia Many rare woods are to be found in the highlands. Unwooded regions are those where elephants and rhinoceros gather and breed. Exotic birds and strange animals abound. The most sought-after products are the feathers of the kingfisher, elephant tusks, rhinoceros horns, and beeswax.

Trade In Cambodia it is the women who take charge of trade. For this reason a Chinese arriving in the country, loses no time in getting himself a mate, for he will find her commercial instincts a great asset.

Utensils For sleeping only bamboo mats are used, laid on the wooden floors. Of late, certain families have adopted the use of low beds, which for the most part are made by the Chinese.

Notes on the customs of Cambodia was translated from the Chinese original into French by Paul Pelliot. J Gilman d'Arcy Paul translated the French version into English, and the Siam Society in Bangkok have republished this version with colour photographs and reproductions of Delaporte's fine lithographs of the monuments. The *Customs of Cambodia*, Siam Society: Bangkok, 1993.

inscription says 'the deer is its food', an artistic directive, which the carver obviously forgot to remove. The other bas-reliefs give an insight into Khmer life at the time: the warrior elephants, oxcarts, fishing with nets, cockfights and skewered fish drying on racks; vignettes show musicians, jugglers, hunters, chess-players, people nit-picking hair, palm readers and reassuringly down-to-earth scenes of Angkor citizens enjoying a drink. In the naval battle scenes, the water around the war canoes is depicted by the presence of fish, crocodiles and floating corpses.

Royal Enclosure

The Royal Enclosure, to the north of the Bayon, had already been laid out by Suryavarman I: the official palace was in the front with the domestic quarters behind, its gardens surrounded by a laterite wall and moat. Suryavarman I also beautified the royal city with ornamental pools. Jayavarman VII simply improved his designs.

Terrace of the elephants In front of the Royal Enclosure, at the centre of Angkor Thom, Suryavarman I laid out the first Grand Plaza with the recently renovated Terrace of the Elephants (also called the Royal Terrace). The 300-m-long wall derives its name from the large, lifelike carvings of elephants in a hunting scene, adorning its walls. The 2.5-m wall also features elephants flanking the southern stairway. Believed to once be the foundations for the royal reception hall, lead tiles were found here in more recent years. This discovery corroborates Chinese diplomat Chou Ta-kuan's evidence that "the tiles of the king's main apartment are made of lead". Royalty once sat in gold-topped pavilions at the centre of the pavilion, and here there are rows of garudas (bird-men), their wings lifted as if in flight. They were intended to give the impression that the god-king's palace was floating in the heavens like the imagined flying celestial palaces of the gods. At the end of the terrace is an impressive sculpture of a five-headed horse.

North and South Kleangs Also in front of the Royal Enclosure are the stately North and South Kleangs, which sit on the east side of the central square (opposite the Terrace of the Elephants). Although Kleang means 'storeroom', a royal oath of allegiance carved into one of the doorways indicates that they may have served as reception areas for foreign envoys. The North Kleang was originally constructed in wood under Rajendravarman II; Jayavarman V reconstructed it with stone and Jayavarman VII later added 12 laterite victory towers, called the **Prasat Suor Prat**. The function of the towers is steeped in controversy. While some say they were intended as anchors for performing acrobats and clowns, Chou Ta-kuan stated that they were used to settle disputes between performing men (to see who could last the longest seated on a tower without illness or injury). Henri Mauhot disagreed with both theories, suggesting that the towers were created to hold the crown jewels.

Terrace of the Leper King At the northeast corner of the 'central square' is the 12th-century Terrace of the Leper King, which may have been a cremation platform for the aristocracy of Angkor. Now rebuilt it is a little too fresh and contemporary for some tastes. The 7-m-high double terrace has bands of bas-reliefs, one on top of the other, with intricately sculptured scenes of royal pageantry and seated apsaras as well as nagas and garudas which frequented the slopes of Mount Meru. Above is a strange statue from an earlier date, which probably depicts the god of death, Yama, and once held a staff in its right hand. The statue's naked, lichen-covered body gives the terrace its name – the lichen gives the uncanny impression of leprosy.

Opposite the Terrace of the Elephants, on the south side of the Terrace of the Leper King, are the remains of an earlier wall, carved with bas-reliefs of demons. These reliefs were found by French archaeologists and had been intentionally concealed. This illustrates the lengths to which the Khmers went to recreate Mount Meru (the home of the gods) as faithfully as possible. According to Hindu mythology, Mount Meru extended into the bowels of the earth; the bas-relief section below ground level was carved with weird and wonderful creatures to symbolize the hidden depths of the underworld. The second layer of carving is the base of Mount Meru on earth. Flights of steps led through these to the lawns and pavilions of the royal gardens and Suryavarman's palace.

The Phimeanakas

The Phimeanakas (meaning Celestial or Flying Palace in Sanskrit) inside the Royal Enclosure was started by Rajendravarman and used by all the later kings. The structure stands close to the walls of the Royal Palace, none of which exists today. Suryavarman I rebuilt this pyramidal temple when he was renovating the Royal Enclosure. It rises from the centre of the former royal palace. Lions guard all four stairways to the central tower which was originally covered in gold, as the Chinese envoy Chou Ta-kuan related in 1296 (for Chou Ta-kuan's account, see page 24). The Phimeanakas represented a genuine architectural revolution: it was not square, but rectangular and on the upper terrace, surrounding the central tower, there was a gallery with corbelled vaults, used as a passageway.

The Srah Srei, or the women's bath, to the north of Phimeanakas is also within the walled enclosure. Chou Ta-kuan appears to have enjoyed watching Angkor's womenfolk bathe, noting that, "To enter the water, the women simply hide their sex with their left hand". The Phimeanakas is linked by the **Avenue of Victory** to the Eastern Baray.

South of the Royal Enclosure

South of the Royal Enclosure and near the Terrace of the Elephants is the Baphuon, built by Udayadityavarman II. The temple was approached by a 200-m-long sandstone causeway, raised on pillars, which was probably constructed after the temple was built. The platform leads from the temple-mountain itself to the east gopura – an arched gateway leading to the temple courtyards. The Baphuon is not well preserved as it was erected on an artificial hill which weakened its foundations. Only the three terraces of its pyramidal, Mount Meru-style form remain and these give little indication of its former glory: it was second only to the Bayon in size. Chou Ta-kuan reported that its great tower was made of bronze and that it was "truly marvellous to behold". With extensive restoration, the temple is starting to shape-up. Most of the bas-reliefs were carved in panels and refer to the Hindu epics. Some archaeologists believe the sculptors were trying to tell stories in the same way as the shadow plays. It is believed that the fourth level wall on the western side was originally created in the form of a large, reclining Buddha, though it is hard to make out today. There is a wonderful view from the summit. South of the Baphuon returns you back to the Bayon.

Preah Palilay

Preah Palilay, just outside the north wall of the Royal Enclosure, was also built by Jayavarman VII. Just to the east of this temple is **Tep Tranam**, the base of a pagoda, with a pool in front of it. To the east of Tep Tranam and the other side of the Northern Avenue is the **Preah Pithu Group**, a cluster of five temples.

South of Angkor Thom

elephants take tourists up to the summit of Phnom Bakheng for sunset

Phnom Bakheng and Baksei Chamkrong

To get up to the ruins, either climb the steep and uneven hill where the vegetation has been cleared (slippery when wet), ride an elephant to the top of the hill (US$15) or walk up the gentle zig-zag path the elephants take.

Phnom Bakheng, Yasovarman's temple-mountain, stands at the top of a natural hill, 60-m high, affording good views of the plains of Angkor. There is also a roped off Buddha's footprint to see. It is just outside the south gate of Angkor Thom and was the centre of King Yasovarman's city, Yasodharapura – the 'City Endowed with Splendour'. A pyramid-temple dedicated to Siva, Bakheng was the home of the royal lingam and Yasovarman's mausoleum after his death. It is composed of five towers built on a sandstone platform. There are 108 smaller towers scattered around the terraces. The main tower has been partially demolished and the others have completely disappeared. It was entered via a steep flight of steps which were guarded by squatting lions. The steps have deteriorated with the towers. Foliate scroll relief carving covers much of the main shrine – the first time this style was used. This strategically placed hill served as a camp for various combatants, including the Vietnamese, and suffered accordingly. Today the hill is disfigured by a radio mast.

Baksei Chamkrong was built by Harshavarman I at the beginning of the 10th century and dedicated to his father, Yasovarman I. It lies at the foot of Phnom Bakheng (between Bakheng and Angkor Thom), the centre of Yasovarman's city, and was one of the first temples to be built in brick on a stepped laterite base. An inscription tells of a golden image of Siva inside the temple.

Chau Say Tevoda and Thommanon

There is a close group of temples just outside the east gate of Angkor Thom. **Chau Say Tevoda**, built by Suryavarman II, is the first temple outside the east gate and is dwarfed by Ta Keo. The temple is dedicated to Siva but many of the carvings are of Vishnu. It is similar in plan to **Thommanon**, next door, whose surrounding walls have completely disappeared, leaving only the gateways on the east and west ends and a ruined central tower. Originally both temples would have had a hall linked to the central tower and enclosing walls with elaborate gateways. A library, to the southeast, is the only other building in the complex. There are repeated pediments above the doorways.

Ta Keo and Ta Nei

Ta Keo, begun during Jayavarman V's reign and left unfinished, stands east of the Royal Palace and just off the Avenue of Victory. The pyramid-temple rises over 50 m, its five tower shrines supported on a five-tiered pyramid. It was one of the first temples to be built entirely of sandstone. Previous tower sanctuaries had entrances only on the east side but Ta Keo has openings on all four sides. It was originally surrounded by a moat.

Deeper in the forest, 600 m north of Ta Keo, is **Ta Nei**. Built by Jayavarman VII the building has appropriated the Bayon's style but on a much smaller scale. Much of the building still remains in the collapsed state but ongoing work from the Apsara Authority means the building is being used for training purposes. It is an overgrown temple with lichen-covered bas-reliefs.

★Ta Prohm

For all would-be Mouhots and closet Indiana Joneses, the temple of Ta Prohm, to the south of Ta Keo, is the perfect lost-in-the-jungle experience. Unlike most of the other monuments at Angkor, it has only been minimally cleared of undergrowth, fig trees and creepers and so retains much of its mystery. Widely regarded as one of Angkor's most enchanting and beautiful temples, it is an absolute 'must-see'.

Ta Prohm was built to house the divine image of the Queen Mother and was consecrated in 1186 – five years after Jayavarman VII seized power. The outer enclosures are somewhat obscured by dense foliage but reach well beyond the temple's heart (1 km by 650 m). The temple proper consists of a number of concentric galleries featuring corner towers and the standard gopuras. Other buildings and enclosures were built on a more ad hoc basis. The temple marked the end of an architectural style in which the temple's structure lay on a single plane with rising towers alluding to the notion of elevation rather than comprising multiple levels.

It underwent many transformations and an inscription gives detailed information on the complex. Within the complex walls lived 12,640 citizens. It contained 39 sanctuaries or prasats, 566 stone dwellings and 288 brick dwellings. Ta Prohm literally translates as the Royal Monastery and that is what it functioned as, home to

ANGKOR
Motifs in Khmer sculpture

The **kala** is a jawless monster commanded by the gods to devour his own body – it made its first appearance in lintels at Roluos. The monster represented devouring time and was an early import from Java.

Singhas (below, left) or lions appeared in stylized forms and are often guardians to temples. The lions lack realism probably because the carvers had never seen one.

The **makara** was a mythical water monster with a scaley body, eagles' talons and an elephantine trunk.

The **naga** (below, right) or sacred snakes play an important part in Hindu mythology and the Khmers drew on them for architectural inspiration. Possibly more than any other single symbol or motif, the naga is characteristic of Southeast Asia. The naga is an aquatic serpent, the word being Sanskrit for snake, and is intimately associated with water (a key component of Khmer prosperity). In Hindu mythology the naga coils beneath and supports Vishnu on the cosmic ocean. The snake also swallows the waters of life, these only being set free to reinvigorate the world after Indra ruptures the serpent with a bolt of lightning. Another version has Vishnu's servants pulling at the serpent to squeeze the waters of life from it (the so-called churning of the sea). The naga permeates Southeast Asian life from royalty to villager. The bridge across the Bayon to Angkor Wat features nagas churning the oceans; men in Vietnam, Laos

Singha

Naga

and Thailand used to tattoo their bodies with nagas for protection; water, the gift of life in a region where wet rice is the staple crop, is measured in Thailand in terms of numbers of nagas; while objects from boats to water storage jars to temples to musical instruments are decorated with the naga motif throughout Southeast Asia.

The **garuda** (below, left) appeared relatively late in Khmer architecture. This mythical creature – half man, half bird – was the vehicle of the Hindu god, Vishnu and the sworn enemy of the nagas.

The **apsaras** (below, right) are regarded as one of the greatest invention of the Khmers. The gorgeous temptresses – born, according to legend, 'during the churning of the Sea of Milk' – were Angkor's equivalent of pin-up girls and represented the ultimate ideal of feminine beauty. They lived in heaven where their sole raison d'être was to have eternal sex with Khmer heroes and holy men. The apsaras are carved with splendidly ornate jewellery and, clothed in the latest Angkor fashion, they strike seductive poses and seemingly compete with each other like models on a catwalk. Different facial features suggest the existence of several races at Angkor – it is possible that they might be modelled on women captured in war. Together with the five towers of Angkor Wat they have become the symbol of Khmer culture. The god-king himself possessed an apsara-like retinue of court dancers – impressive enough for Chinese envoy Chou Ta-kuan to write home about it in in 1296 (see page 24).

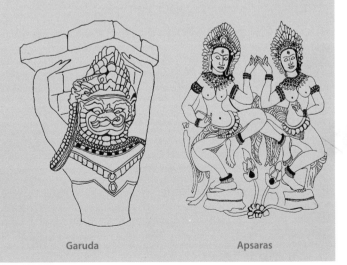

Garuda   Apsaras

18 abbots and 2740 monks. By the 12th century temples were no longer exclusively places of worship – they also had to accommodate monks so roofed halls were increasingly built within the complexes. According to contemporary inscriptions, the temple required 79,365 people for its upkeep, relying on the income of 3140 villages to subsidize the 2740 officials and 615 dancers. The list of property it owned was on an equally impressive scale. It included 523 parasols, 35 diamonds and 40,620 pearls.

The French writer Elie Lauré wrote: "With its millions of knotted limbs, the forest embraces the ruins with a violent love". Creepers entwine themselves around ancient stones like the tentacles of a giant octopus. Trunks and roots pour off temple roofs like lava flows. It was decided by the École Française d'Extrême Orient to leave the temple in its natural state. The trees are predominantly the silk-cotton tree and the aptly named strangler fig. The plants are believed to have spawned in the temple's cracks from seeds blown in or dropped by birds. Naturally, the roots of the trees have descended towards the soil, prying their way through foundations in the process. As the vegetation has matured it has forced its way further into the temple's structure, damaging the man-built base and causing untold destruction. This has created a situation where the structures now rely on the trees for support. Herein lies the dilemma – if the trees die or are damaged, the now-damaged and loose temple walls could easily crumble or collapse. Venerable trees weighing several tonnes growing on temple roofs also cause unimaginable stress, slowly shattering the stones.

In recent years a colossal tree was struck by lightening and fell on a gallery, causing quite serious damage. This reignited a campaign to 'save Ta Prohm' and a project is underway to prune some of the smaller trees and larger branches.

Banteay Kdei, Srah Srang and Prasat Kravan

Banteay Kdei The massive complex of Banteay Kdei, otherwise known as 'the citadel of cells', is 3 km east of Angkor Thom and just to the southeast of Ta Prohm. Some archaeologists think it may be dedicated to Jayavarman VII's religious teacher. The temple has remained in much the same state it was discovered in – a crowded collection of ruined laterite towers and connecting galleries lying on a flat plan, surrounded by a galleried enclosure. It is presumed that the temple was a Buddhist monastery and hundreds of buried Buddha statues have been excavated from the site. In recent times a community of monks has used the site but this is less common now due to the strict restrictions imposed by temple management. The temple area is enclosed by a large laterite wall, 700 m by 500 m, and has three main enclosures. Like Ta Prohm it contains a Hall of Dancers (east side), an open roof building with four separate quarters. The second enclosure runs around the perimeters of the inner enclosure. The third, inner enclosure contains a north and south library and central sanctuary. The central tower was never finished and the square pillars in the middle of the courtyard still cannot be explained by scholars. There are few inscriptions here to indicate either its name or purpose, but it is almost certainly a Buddhist temple built in the 12th century, about the same time as Ta Prohm. It is quite similar to Ta Prohm in design but on a much smaller scale.

Historians Freeman and Jacques believe that it was probably built over the site of another temple. The temple is being restored, slowly but surely. However, the 13th-century vandalism of Buddha images (common to most of Jayavarman's temples) will prove a little more difficult to restore. This temple offers a few good examples of Mahayanist Buddhist frontons and lintels that escaped the desecration.

Srah Srang The lake or baray next to Banteay Kdei is called Srah Srang ('Royal Bath') and was used for ritual bathing. The steps down to the water face the rising sun and are flanked with lions and nagas. This sandstone landing stage dates from the reign of Jayavarman VII but the lake itself is thought to date back two centuries earlier. A 10th-century inscription reads "this water is stored for the use of all creatures except dyke breakers", ie elephants. This design is believed to be characteristic of that adopted in the Bayon. The Baray, which measures 700 m by 300 m, has been filled with turquoise-blue waters for over 1300 years. With a good view of Pre Rup across the lake, some archaeologists believe that this spot affords the best vista in the whole Angkor complex. The green landscape around the baray and beautiful views offer a tranquil and cool resting place, perfect for a picnic lunch.

Prasat Kravan On the road between Angkor Wat and Banteay Kdei, on the small circuit, is Prasat Kravan. The temple, built in AD 921, means 'Cardamom Sanctuary' and is unusual in that it is built of brick. (By that time brick had been replaced by laterite and sandstone.) It consists of five brick towers arranged in a line. The bricklayers did a good job, especially considering they used a vegetable composite as their mortar. The temple's bas-reliefs are considered a bit of an anomaly as brick was hardly ever sculpted upon. In the early 10th century, temples were commissioned by individuals other than the king; Prasat Kravan is one of the earliest examples. It was probably built during the reign of Harshavarman I.

The Hindu temple, surrounded by a moat, is positioned in a north-south direction. Two of the five decorated brick towers contain bas-reliefs (the north and central towers). The central tower is probably the most impressive and contains a linga on a pedestal. The sanctuary's three walls all contain pictures of Vishnu; the left-hand wall depicts Vishnu disguised as Vamana the dwarf. The incarnation of Vamana was used to dupe the evil demon king, Bali, into letting the unassuming dwarf take a small space to meditate. Instead the mighty Vishnu rose up, taking three important steps – from a pedestal, across the ocean, to a lotus – in order to reclaim the world from the evil demon king. On the right-hand wall again is the mighty Vishnu riding his Garuda. Common to both the bas-reliefs is the four-armed Vishnu waving around a number of objects: disc, club, conch shell and ball – these are all symbolic of his personal attributes and power. On the opposing wall is Vishnu, this time with eight arms standing between six rows of people meditating above a giant reptile.

The Northern tower is devoted to Lakshimi, Vishnu's wife. Like her consort, she is also baring her personal attributes. The best light to view the relief is in the morning.

The Cardamom Sanctuary is named after a tree that grew on the grounds. Ironically, its ruin has been largely due to the roots of trees growing beneath it. The

French have been involved in the temple's reconstruction. The temple's twin, Prasat Neang Khamau (the Black Lady Sanctuary), can be found outside Phnom Penh.

Pre Rup

Northeast of Srah Srang is Pre Rup, the State Temple of King Rajendravarman's capital. Built in AD 961, the temple-mountain representing Mount Meru is larger, higher and artistically superior than its predecessor, the East Mebon, which it closely resembles. In keeping with the tradition of state capitals, Pre Rup marked the centre of the city, much of which doesn't exist today. The pyramid-structure, which is constructed of laterite with brick prasats, sits at the apex of an artificial, purpose-built mountain. The temple is enclosed by a laterite outer wall (127 m by 117 m) and inner wall (87 m by 77 m) both which contain gopuras in the centre of each wall. The central pyramid-level consists of a three-tiered, sandstone platform, with five central towers sitting above. This was an important innovation at Pre Rup and East Mebon, that the sanctuary at the top was no longer a single tower – but a group of five towers, surrounded by smaller towers on the outer, lower levels. This more complicated plan reached its final development at Angkor Wat 150 years later. The group of five brick towers were originally elaborately decorated with plaster, but most of it has now fallen off. However, the corners of each of the five towers contain guardian figures – as per tradition, the eastern towers are female and the western and central towers are male. The shrine has fine lintels and columns on its doorways. But the intricate sandstone carvings on the doors of the upper levels are reproductions. The upper levels of the pyramid offer a brilliant, panoramic view of the countryside.

Eastern Baray, East Mebon and Banteay Samre

Eastern Baray Built by Yasovarman I and fed by the Siem Reap River, the Eastern Baray – or Baray Orientale – is a large reservoir (7 km by 1.8 km), now dried up, that was the labour of love for Yasovarman I. Historian Dawn Rooney believes it took 6000 workers more than three years to complete. The baray was Yasovarman I's first major work. To keep the punters on side he needed to provide a reliable water supply to his new kingdom, Yasodharataka. And that he did. At full capacity the baray could hold around 45-50 million cubic metres of water. He named the baray Yasodharataka and declared it protected by the goddess Ganga (overseen by abbots from the ashramas south of the baray). The four corners are marked by stelae.

East Mebon Today, a boat isn't required to reach the middle of the Eastern Baray, where the flamboyant five towers of the East Mebon are located. Intrepid traveller Helen Churchill Candee remarked of the temple: "Could any conception be lovelier, a vast expanse of sky-tinted water as wetting for a perfectly ordered temple."

The Hindu pyramid structure consists of three tiers. Guarding the corners of the first and second levels are carefully sculpted elephants and sculptures (the best one is in the southeast corner). The inner enclosure contains eight smaller towers and skilfully carved lintels upon the gopuras featuring Lakshmi being watered down by two elephants and Vishnu in his man-lion guise, Narasimha. The upper terrace contains the five towers, the northwest tower features Ganesha riding his own trunk; the southeast tower shows an elephant being eaten by a monster and the central sanctuary's lintels depict Indra on his mount and Varuna the Guardian.

Finished in AD 952, Rajendravarman seems to have followed the Roluos trend and dedicated East Mebon to his parents. The East Mebon and Pre Rup were the last monuments in plaster and brick; they mark the end of a Khmer architectural epoch. The overall temple construction utilizes all materials that were available at the time: plaster, brick, laterite and sandstone. Although many believe East Mebon to be a temple-mountain, that wasn't its original intention, it just appears that way now that surrounding waters have disappeared. The Siem Reap River is said to have been diverted while the temple was built.

Banteay Samre Further to the east, around 500 m past the east end of the East Baray, Banteay Samre is a Hindu temple dedicated to Vishnu, although reliefs decorating some of the frontons (the triangular areas above arches) portray Buddhist scenes. It is thought to have been built by Suryavarman II and has many characteristics of Angkor Wat such as stone-vaulted galleries and a high central tower. The bas-reliefs are in fine condition.

North of Angkor Thom

head north for Jayavarman VII's first capital

Preah Khan

Northeast of the walled city of Angkor Thom, about 3.5 km from the Bayon, is the 12th-century complex of Preah Khan. One of the largest complexes within the Angkor area, it was Jayavarman VII's first capital before Angkor Thom was completed. The name Preah Khan means 'sacred sword' and probably derives from a decisive battle against the Cham, which created a 'lake of blood', but was inevitably won by Jayavarman VII.

Preah Khan is not uniform in style. It is highly likely that Jayavarman VII's initial very well-organized and detailed city plans went slightly pear-shaped during the working city's life. A number of alterations and buildings were added, in addition to a vast civilian habitation (huts and timber houses), which all came together to create a complex labyrinth of architectural chaos. It is similar in ground plan to Ta Prohm (see page 29) but attention was paid to the approaches: its east and west entrance avenues, leading to ornamental causeways, are lined with carved stone boundary posts. Evidence of 1000 teachers suggests that it was more than a mere Buddhist monastery but most likely a Buddhist university. Nonetheless an abundance of Brahmanic iconography is still present on site. Around the rectangular complex is a large laterite wall surrounded by large garudas wielding the naga (each over 5 m in height). The theme continues across the length of the whole 3-km external enclosure, with the motif dotted every 50 m. Within these walls lies the surrounding moat.

The city is conveniently located on the shores of its own baray, Jayataka (3.5 km by 900 m). Some foundations and laterite steps lead from the reservoir, where two beautiful gajasimha lions guard the path. It is best to enter the temple from the baray's jetty in order to experience the magnificence of the divinities and devas of the Processional Way (causeway leading across the moat).

The construction's four walls meet in the centre creating two galleries and likewise, two enclosures. The outer enclosure contains the traditional four gopuras (adorned with stately bas-reliefs) and the Hall of Dancers. This hall contains an elaborate frieze of dancing apsaras and was used, in recent times, to host charity performances to help fund the area's restoration. Within the enclosure there are also a few ponds, libraries and supplementary buildings, most notably, a two-storey pavilion (north of the performance hall) which is believed to have housed the illustrious 'sacred sword'.

The second and innermost walls run so closely together that it is possible to pass through the following enclosure without realizing you had entered it (this is probably due to an expansion undertaken very early on in the piece to offer additional protection to the shrines).

The inner enclosure is a bewildering array of constructions and shrines. Holes in the inner walls of the central sanctuary of Preah Khan suggest they may once have been decorated with brass plates – an obvious target for looters. One inscription implies that up to 1500 tonnes was used within the edifice. The temple was built to shelter the statue of Jayavarman VII's father, Dharanindravarman II, in the likeness of Bodhisattva Avatokitsvara, which has now probably been smashed. A stela was

Preah Khan

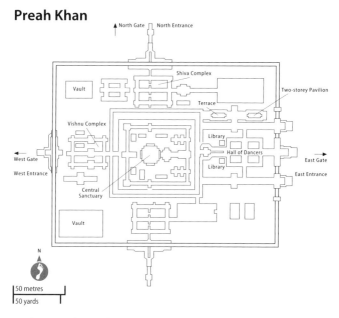

discovered at the site glorifying the builder, Jayavarman VII and detailing what it took to keep the place ticking over. The inventory mentions that for Preah Khan's upkeep, the services of 97,840 men and women, 444 chefs, 4606 footmen and 2298 servants were required. Preah Khan's inscriptions also refer to the existence of 515 other statues, 102 royal hospitals of the kingdom, 18 major annual festivals and 10 days' public holiday a month.

The temple was starting to deteriorate, but clearing and careful conservation have helped remedy this. During the dry season, the World Monuments Funds (WMF), based in New York, undertakes archaeological site conservation activities here.

Preah Neak Pean, Ta Som and Krol Ko
To the east of Preah Khan and north of the Eastern Baray are two more Buddhist temples built by Jayavarman VII: Preah Neak Pean (the westernmost one) and the ruins of Ta Som.

Neak Pean This exquisite temple was also a fountain, built in the middle of a pool, representing the paradisiacal Himalayan mountain-lake, Anaavatapta. Two nagas form the edge of the island and their tails join at the back. In modern Khmer it is known as the Prea-sat neac pon – the 'tower of the intertwined dragons'. The colossal image of the horse is the compassionate Bodhisattva who is supposed to save sailors from drowning. The temple pools were an important part of the aesthetic experience of Preah Khan and Neak Pean – the ornate stone carving of both doubly visible by reflection. Such basins within a temple complex were used for religious ritual, while the larger moats and barays were used for bathing, transport and possibly for irrigation.

Ta Som Located north of the East Baray is the pretty Ta Som. This mini temple has many of the same stylistic and design attributes of Ta Prohm and Banteay Kdei but on a much smaller scale. Unlike the larger constructions of Jayavarman VII, Ta Som's layout is extremely simple – three concentric enclosures and very few annex buildings. The main entrance is to the east, which would indicate some urbanization on the eastern side of the temple. The two inner enclosures are successively offset to the west. The outer (third) enclosure (240 m x 200 m) is pierced by two cruciform gopuras; the eastern one is preceded by a small terrace bound by naga balustrades. The current entry is through the western gopura as this faces the road between East Mebon and Preah Neak Pean and cuts across the moat.

Krol Ko North of Preah Neak Pean and about 2 km past Ta Som, Krol Ko was built in the late 12th to early 13th century. Referred to as the Oxen Park, Krol Ko is a single, laterite tower which is about 30 m sq. The two frontons represent bodhisattva Lokesvara, to whom it is believed the temple is dedicated.

Western Baray, West Mebon and Ak Thom
Take Highway 6 west. About 3 km west of the airport turning a track leads north. It is 4 km from Highway 6 to Western Baray. Boats can be hired from the beach on the south of the Western Baray. The boat trip to West Mebon takes about 15 mins.

The **Western Baray** was built by Udayaditavarman II possibly to increase the size of the irrigated farmlands. In the centre, on an island, is the **West Mebon**, where the famous bronze statue of Vishnu was discovered (now in the National Museum at Phnom Penh). Today, the eastern end of the Western Baray is dry but the scale remains astonishing, more than 2 km across and 9 km long with an average depth of 7 m. It is believed that the reservoir could hold around 123 million cubic litres of water.

South of the Western Baray is **Ak Thom**, marking the site of Jayavarman II's earlier city. It is the oldest surviving temple in the Angkor region and although little remains, it is worth a visit. The central towers are constructed mostly of brick cemented together with a mortar of vegetable sap, palm sugar and termite soil.

The Roluos Group
The Roluos Group, some 16 km southeast of Siem Reap, receives few visitors but is worth visiting if time permits. Jayavarman II built several capitals including one at Roluos, at that time called Hariharalaya. This was the site of his last city and remained the capital during the reigns of his three successors. The three remaining Hindu sanctuaries at Roluos are **Preah Ko**, **Bakong** and **Lolei**. They were finished in AD 879, AD 881 and AD 893 respectively by Indravarman I and his son Yashovarman I and are the best preserved of the early temples.

All three temples are built of brick with sandstone doorways and niches. The use of human figures as sculptural decoration in religious architecture developed around this time – and examples of these guardian spirits can be seen in the niches of Preah Ko and Lolei. Other sculptured figures which appear in the Roluos Group are the crouching lion, the reclining bull (Nandi – Siva's mount) and the naga. The gopura – an arched gateway leading to the temple courtyards – was also a contemporary innovation in Roluos. Libraries used for the storage of sacred manuscripts appeared for the first time, as did the concentric enclosures surrounding the central group of towers. Preah Ko and Lolei have characteristics in common: both were dedicated to the parents and grandparents of the kings who built them. Neither temple has a pyramid centre like Bakong as the pyramid temples were built exclusively for kings.

Preah Ko Meaning 'sacred ox', Preah Ko was named after the three statues of Nandi (the mount of the Hindu god, Siva) which stand in front of the temple.

Orientated east-west, there is a cluster of six brick towers arranged in two rows on a low brick platform, the steps up to which are guarded by crouching lions while Nandi, looking back, blocks the way. The front row of towers was devoted to Indravarman's male ancestors and the second row to the female. The ancestors were represented in the image of a Hindu god. Only patches remain of the once magnificent stucco relief work, including a remnant of a kala – a motif also found on contemporary monuments in Java.

Tip...
It is possible to visit the other ancient Khmer sites dotted around the main temples at Angkor; most can be reached by moto or by car.

Bakong Indravarman's temple-mountain, Bakong, is a royal five-stepped pyramid temple with a sandstone central tower built on a series of successively receding terraces with surrounding brick towers. It may have been inspired by Borobudur in Java. Indravarman himself was buried in the temple. Bakong is the largest and most impressive temple in the Roluos Group by a long way. A bridge flanked by a naga balustrade leads over a dry moat to the temple. The central tower was built to replace the original one when the monument was restored in the 12th century and is probably larger than the original. Local children will point out to you that it is just possible to catch a glimpse of Angkor Wat from the top. The Bakong denotes the true beginning of classical Khmer architecture and contained the god-king Siva's lingam. The most important innovations of Indravarman's artists are the free-standing sandstone statues – such as the group of three figures, probably depicting the king with his two wives, who are represented as Siva with Uma, a Hindu goddess and consort of Siva, and Ganga, goddess of the Ganges River. The corners of the pyramid are mounted with statues of elephants and the steps guarded by crouching lions. Nandi watches the steps from below. The heads of all the figures are now missing but the simplicity of the sculpture is nonetheless distinctive; it is a good example of early Khmer craftsmanship. The statues are more static and stockier than the earlier statues of Chenla. There is now a Buddhist monastery in the grounds – originally it was dedicated to Siva.

Lolei Built by Yashovarman I in the middle of Indravarman's baray, Lolei's brick towers were dedicated to the king's ancestors, but over the centuries they have largely disintegrated; of the four towers two have partly collapsed. Much of the decoration has worn away but the inscriptions carved in the grey sandstone lintels and door jambs remain in good condition.

Phnom Krom and Phnom Bok
Phnom Krom Today, Phnom Krom, 12 km southwest of Siem Reap, is the base for nearby boat trips out to the Tonlé Sap's floating villages. However, at the top of the 140-m-high mountain, stands a ruined temple believed to have been built in the late 9th-10th century by Yasovarman I but there are no inscriptions giving exact details. The square laterite enclosure (50 m by 50 m) features a gopura in the middle of each outer wall and includes 10 halls, now mostly crumbled, that make an almost continuous inner square. On a lower platform are three stone sanctu-

ary towers, aligned north to south, dedicated to Shiva, Vishnu and Brahma. The temple affords amazing 360-degree panoramic views, which extend across to the Western Baray and Tonlé Sap's floating villages.

Phnom Bok Brother temple to Phnom Krom, the two temples feature almost an identical layout. The carvings and decorative features here remain in far better condition due to their more protected location and relatively recent discovery. Approximately 15 km northwest of Siem Riep, the temple sits at the pinnacle of the 235-m-high hill. It is the most elevated of the three temple peaks of Angkor; with Phnom Krom at 137 m and Phnom Bakheng at only 60 m (the hill that is climbed the most by tourists being by far the smallest). All three temples were built by Yasovarman I; Phnom Bakheng was the first.

The ascent of Phnom Bok is a difficult climb but well rewarded, as the 20- to 30-minute hike up the southern slope reveals a limitless horizon, broken only to the north by the view of Phnom Kulen.

★Banteay Srei ('Citadel of Women')
25 km from Ta Prohm along a decent road and about 35-40 mins by motorbike. The way is well signed. There are lots of food and drink stalls.

Banteay Srei, to the north of Angkor, is well worth the trip. This remarkable temple was built by the Brahmin tutor to King Rajendravarman, Yajnavaraha, grandson of Harshavarman (AD 900-923), and founded in AD 967. The temple wasn't discovered until 1914, its distance from Angkor and concealment by overgrown jungle meaning that it wasn't picked up in earlier expeditions. At the time of discovery, by geographic officer Captain Marec, the site was so badly damaged that mounds of dirt had covered the main structure and foliage had bored its way through much of the site. It wasn't until 1924 that the site was cleared and by 1936 it had been restored.

Banteay Srei

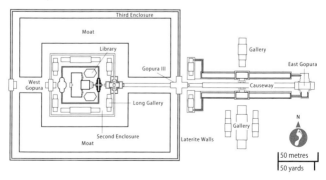

Banteay Srei translates as 'Citadel of Women', a title bestowed upon it in relatively recent years due to the intricate apsara carvings that adorn the interior. While many of Angkor's temples are impressive because of their sheer size, Banteay Srei stands out in the quality of its craftsmanship. The temple is considered by many historians to be the highest achievement of art from the Angkor period. The explicit preservation of this temple reveals covered terraces, of which only the columns remain, which once lined both sides of the primary entrance. In keeping with tradition, a long causeway leads into the temple, across a moat, on the eastern side.

The main walls, entry pavilions and libraries have been constructed from laterite and the carvings are in pink sandstone. The layout was inspired by Prasat Thom at Koh Ker. Three beautifully carved tower-shrines stand side by side on a low terrace in the middle of a quadrangle, with a pair of libraries on either side enclosed by a wall. Two of the shrines, the southern one and the central one, were dedicated to Siva and the northern one to Vishnu. Both had libraries close by, with carvings depicting appropriate legends. The whole temple is dedicated to Brahma and many believe this temple is the closest to its Indian counterparts. Beyond this inner group of buildings was a monastery surrounded by a moat.

In 1923 controversy surrounded the temple when it was targeted by famous French author André Lalraux for a major looting expedition. The author of *The Royal Way* (1930) shamefully attempted to pillage Banteay Srei of its treasures, having read that the temple not only contained a series of brilliant carvings in excellent condition but that it was also unexcavated (which he took to mean abandoned). He travelled to Angkor and proceeded to cut out one tonne of the finest statues and bas-reliefs. Fortunately, he was arrested trying to leave the country with the treasures and was sentenced to three years in prison (a term that he did not serve). One of the best known statues from this site is a sculpture of Siva sitting down and holding his wife, Uma, on his knee: it is in the National Museum of Arts in Phnom Penh.

Having been built by a Brahmin priest, the temple was never intended for use by a king, which goes some way towards explaining its small size – you have to duck to get through the doorways to the sanctuary towers. Perhaps because of its modest scale Banteay Srei contains some of the finest examples of Khmer sculpture. Finely carved pink sandstone ornaments, roofs, pediments and lintels, all magnificently decorated with tongues of flame, serpents' tails, gods, demons and floral garlands.

Phnom Kulen

It takes a good 2 hrs by moto to get to Phnom Kulen from Siem Reap; it is more than 1 hr beyond Banteay Srei. At the height of the wet season the road will be virtually impassable. Entering the park costs foreigners an extra US$20 (or US$12 from the Angkor City Hotel beforehand) plus a fee for a motorbike or car (US$25-30) and it is not covered by the Angkor ticket scheme.

Phnom Kulen – or Mount Mohendrapura – 28 km northeast of Angkor and 48 km from Siem Reap, is a sandstone plateau considered sacred by the Khmers. The site is the mythical birthplace of the Cambodian Kingdom. At the hill's summit is the largest reclining Buddha in the country – over 900 years old. Jayavarman II built his first brick pyramid temple-mountain here – to house the sacred golden Siva-lingam – at the beginning of the ninth century. Today the temple is only visible in fragments although, over a millennium later, the phallic emblem is said to be still on display in the Phnom Kulen complex. The temple is best known for its carved lintels and bas-reliefs. There are also some remains of ninth-century Cham temples in the area.

Today the hill is clothed in forest and the nights here are cold and the days fresh and invigorating. As with most of the other sites on Phnom Kulen it is necessary to have a guide to point them out as they are small and well concealed in the forest. Khmer visitors to the area seem only to be interested in the reclining Buddha.

Phnom Kbal Spean

Kbal Spean is 50 km northeast of Siem Reap and should cost no more than US$10 by moto (last entry 1530). Upon arrival, follow the path for 1.5 km for about 40 mins up the narrow path. The ideal time to visit is at the end of the wet season, when the fast-flowing water gushes around, but doesn't submerge most of the carvings.

The intriguing spot of Kbal Spean is rich in both style and purpose. The name of the river, and the mountain from which it springs, translates loosely to Headwater Bridge, referring to a natural sandstone arch, marking the beginning of the 150 m of carvings, upstream from the bridge. It is the downstream part, from the bridge to the waterfall, that gives the river its Sanskrit name Sahasralinga, 'River of a Thousand Lingas'.

Phnom Kbal Spean is regarded as highly auspicious so it is not surprising that the remarkable 11th-century riverbed rock carvings display a gallery of gods and celestial beings including Vishnu reclining on the serpent Anata, Shiva, Brahman, Lakshmi, Rama and Hanuman. Some of the carvings are submerged by the river, while a few have been hacked away by unscrupulous looters. The visibility of all carvings is really dependent on the time of year.

Downstream from the carvings are thousands of sculpted lingas in the river bed and a large underwater representation of a yoni (womb). The lingas stretch approximately 6 m downstream from the bridge, to 30 m upstream. Carved from the coarse sandstone from the riverbed, some protrude as much as 10 cm from the bed; others have been worn away by the flowing water. Finnish journalist Teppo Turkki, who visited the site for the *Phnom Penh Post*, wrote at the beginning of 1995: "The lingas, some of which date back to the ninth century, are about 25 cm sq and 10 cm deep and lined in a perfect grid pattern. The river runs over them, covering them with about 5 cm of pristine water." He continued: "The holy objects are designed to create a 'power path' for the Khmer kings." More likely the water which would have fed Angkor was being sanctified before it entered the holy arena of the temples. Beyond the series of carvings is a 15-m waterfall to a crystal-clear pool.

Chau Srei Vibol

Turn east off the road from between Phnom Bok and Roluos, about 5 km south of Phnom Bok. Follow the road over several old bridges until you reach the compound of Wat Trach and the laterite wall at the bottom of the hill.

The remote, 11th-century hilltop temple of Chau Srei Vibol is now in ruins but at least three major sandstone structures, a sanctuary and two libraries with decorative carvings, are readily identifiable. A couple of broken lions flank the steep eastern entrance gate.

Whilst viewing this small ruined temple in near silence it's worth reflecting on the building boom that occurred under the reign of Suryavarman I, a highpoint in the Khmer Empire. Suryavarman ruled a huge empire, covering much of southern Vietnam, Thailand, Laos and the Malay Peninsula.

Beng Mealea
Beng Mealea is a full day trip from Siem Reap. There is an entrance fee of US$20.

Beng Mealea, a huge 12th-century temple complex, 40 km east of the Bayon and about 7 km southeast of Phnom Kulen, is completely ruined even though it was built at about the same time as Angkor Wat. Its dimensions are similar but Beng Mealea has no central pyramid. It is widely believed that this temple acted as the 'blueprint' for Angkor. Most of the Buddhist temples built under Jayavarman VII – Preah Khan, Banteay Kdei, Ta Som and Ta Prohm – were modelled after this complex.

Siem Reap

The nearest town to Angkor, Siem Reap is a bustling tourism hub with a growing art and fashion crowd. The town has developed quite substantially in the past few years and, with the blossoming of hotels, restaurants and bars, and is now a pleasant place in its own right. It's a popular base for volunteers, and visitors exhausted by the temple trail might care to while away a morning or afternoon in Siem Reap itself. However, without the temples, it's true to say that few people would ever find themselves here.

Sights

The town is laid out formally and, because there is ample land on which to build, it is pleasantly spacious. Buildings are often set in large overgrown grounds resembling mini-wildernesses. However, hotel building has pretty much kept pace with tourist arrivals and the current level of unprecedented growth and development is set to continue, so this may not be the case in the future. The growth spurt has put a great strain on the city's natural resources.

Old Market This area is the most touristy part of town. There is a sprinkling of guesthouses in this area, recommended for independent travellers and those staying more than two or three days. Otherwise, there's a much greater selection of accommodation just across the river, in the **Wat Bo** area. It's not as crowded as the market area and there is less traffic than the airport road.

> **Tip...**
> In Siem Reap visit the market and buy black peppercorns to take home.

Angkor National Museum ⓘ *on the road to the temples, www.angkornational museum.com, daily 0830-1800, US$12.* The museum is a short walk from the town centre. Due to the high entry fee it is usually empty and it does seem rather incongruous that the artefacts on display here are not actually still in-situ at the temples themselves. Having said that, it isn't a bad museum and you can gather a lot of useful information about the development of Angkor. There are also some intriguing background details such as the 102 hospitals built during the reign of Jayavarman VII and the 1960 boxes of haemorrhoid cream that were part of their annual provisions. There are also some displays on the clothes the average Angkorian wore but it's a shame there isn't more about the daily lives of these ancients.

★ Tonlé Sap

The Tonlé Sap, the Great Lake of Cambodia, is one of the natural wonders of Asia. Uniquely, the 100-km-long Tonlé Sap River, a tributary of the mighty Mekong, reverses its flow and runs uphill for six months of the year. Spring meltwaters in the Himalaya, coupled with seasonal rains, increase the flow of the Mekong to such an extent that some is deflected up the Tonlé Sap River. From June the lake begins to expand until, by the end of the rainy season, it has increased in area four-fold and in depth by up to 12 m. At its greatest extent, the lake occupies nearly a seventh of Cambodia's land area, around 1.5 million ha, making it the largest freshwater lake in Southeast Asia. From November, with the onset of the dry season, the Tonlé Sap River reverses its flow once more and begins to act like a regular tributary – flowing downhill into the Mekong. By February the lake has shrunk to a fraction of its wet-season size and covers 'just' 300,000 ha.

This pattern of expansion and contraction has three major benefits. First, it helps to restrict flooding in the Mekong Delta in Vietnam. Second, it forms the basis for a substantial part of Cambodia's rice production. And third, it supports perhaps the world's largest and richest inland fishery, yielding as much as 10 tonnes of fish per square kilometre. It is thought that four million people depend on the lake for their subsistence and three out of every 4 kg of fish caught in the country come from the Tonlé Sap.

Because of the dramatic changes in the size of the lake some of the fish, such as the 'walking catfish', have evolved to survive several hours out of water, flopping overland to find deeper pools. *Hok yue* – or elephant fish – are renowned as a delicacy well beyond Cambodia's borders. Large-scale commercial fishing is a major occupation from February to May and the fishing grounds are divided into plots and leased out. Recent lack of dredging means the lake is not as deep as it was and fish are tending to swim downstream into the Mekong and Tonlé Sap rivers. The annual flooding covers the surrounding countryside with a layer of moist, nutrient-rich mud which is ideal for rice growing. Farmers grow deep-water rice, long stalked and fast growing – it grows with the rising lake to keep the grain above water and the stem can be up to 6 m long. The lake also houses people, with communities living in floating villages close to the shore.

Chong Khneas ⓘ *boats can be hired and trips to floating villages are offered, expect to pay about US$10-15 per hr; take a moto from Siem Reap (10 km, US$2); boats from Phnom Penh berth at Chong Khnea.* Chong Khneas consist of some permanent buildings but is a largely floating settlement. The majority of the population live in houseboats and most services – including police, health, international aid agencies, retail and karaoke – are all provided on water. A trip around the village is testimony to the ingenuity of people living on this waterway with small kids paddling little tubs to each other's ouses.

Tip...
If you want to visit a school and orphanage, go to Savong's School (savong.com), a genuine success story.

Chong Khneas gets hundreds of visitors every day. For a more authentic, less touristy experience head out a bit further, 25 km east, to the village of **Kompong Phluk**. Costs to get to these villages are pretty high (up to US$50 per person) but are brought down if there are more passengers on the boat. See **Terre Cambodge** or **Two Dragons Guesthouse** under What to do to organize a tour.

Siem Reap

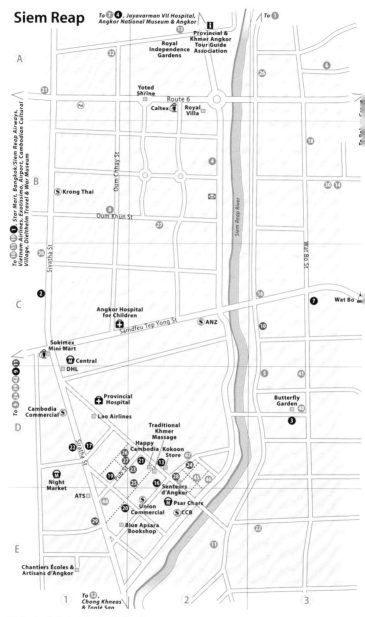

To ⑦ ④, Jayavarman VII Hospital, Angkor National Museum & Angkor

To ①

To ⑩ ⑮ ①, Star Mart, Bangkok/Siem Reap Airways, Vietnam Airlines, Exotissimo, Airport, Cambodian Cultural Village, Diethelm Travel & War Museum

To ⑨ ② ㉓ ⑨ ⑪

Royal Independence Gardens

ℹ Provincial & Khmer Angkor Tour Guide Association

⑬

㉜

⑥

㉑

Yoted Shrine

Route 6

Caltex

Royal Villa

㉖

⑱

Ⓟ Pol

Ⓢ Krong Thai

Oum Chhay St

④

⑧

✉

㉚ ⑭

Oum Khun St

㉗

Sivatha St

㊱

❷

Siem Reap River

Wat Bo St

⑯

❼ Wat Bo

Angkor Hospital for Children

Samdfeu Tep Yong St

Ⓢ ANZ

⑩

Sokimex Mini Mart

Ⓜ Central

DHL

⑤

㊶

Butterfly Garden

㊵

Cambodia Commercial Ⓢ

Ⓟ Provincial Hospital

Lao Airlines

Traditional Khmer Massage

❸

Happy Cambodia

Kokoon Store

㊷

㉖

⑰

㉒

Ⓜ Night Market

⑲

㉓

㉑

⑬

㉘

㉔

㊹ ㊺ ㊻

ATS

㉕

⑯

Senteurs d'Angkor

㊹

㉚

Ⓢ Union Commercial

Ⓜ Psar Chars

㉙

Ⓢ CCB

Blue Apsara Bookshop

㉒

⑪

Chantiers Écoles & Artisans d'Angkor

To ⑫, Chong Khneas & Tonlé Sap

N

100 metres
100 yards

Prek Toal Biosphere Also on the Tonlé Sap Lake is the Prek Toal Biosphere – a bird sanctuary which is home to 120 bird species, including cranes, stalks and pelicans. Boats can be organized from Chong Kneas to visit the Prek Toal Environment Office, US$30 return, one hour. From here you can arrange a guide and another boat for around US$20. **Terre Cambodia**, www.terrecambodge.com, runs boat tours upwards of US$80, as do **Osmose**, T012- 832812, osmose@bigpond.com.kh, and the **Sam Veasna Center for Wildlife and Conservation**, T063-761597, info@samveasna.org. There is basic accommodation at the Environment Office.

Siem Reap listings *map p46*

Tourist information

There is a tourist office at the far end of Sivatha St (towards the crocodile farm), 0730-1100 and 1430-1700.

Where to stay

It is not uncommon for taxi, moto and tuk-tuk drivers to tell new arrivals that the guesthouse they were booked into is now 'closed' or full. They will try to take you to the place where they get the best commission. One way around this is to arrange for the guesthouse or hotel to pick you up from either the bus station or other arrival point – many offer this service for free or a small fee.

$$$$ Angkor Village Resort
1 km north of Siem Reap, Phum Treang, T063-963561, www.angkorvillage.com.
The resort contains 40 rooms set in Balinese-style surroundings. Traditional

massage services, 2 restaurants, theatre shows and lovely pool. Elephant, boat and helicopter rides can be arranged. Recommended.

$$$$ La Résidence d'Angkor Hotel
River Rd, T063-963390, www. residencedangkor.com.
This is a hotel to aspire to. With its beautifully laid out rooms all lavishly furnished with marble and hardwoods, it is reassuringly expensive. Each room has a huge free-form bath – the perfect end to a day touring the temples.

$$$$ Le Meridien Angkor
Main road towards the temples, T063-963900, www.lemeridien.com/angkor.
From the outside this 5-star hotel is severe with angled architecture and small, dark slits for windows. Walk into the lobby and it is immediately transformed into space and light. Rooms are nicely designed and sized and all come with a/c, en suite and cable TV. Other facilities include spa, restaurants and pool. The garden is a lovely spot to take breakfast. Recommended.

$$$$ Park Hyatt Siem Reap
Sivutha Blvd, T063-211234, www. siemreap.park.hyatt.com.
This is probably Siem Reap's best-value luxury hotel. The rooms offer simple contemporary design with giant bathtubs and plump bedding – all with a/c and cable TV. The pool is a maze of plinths and greenery and makes for a perfect spot to laze. Can feel a bit urban for Siem Reap but still a great hotel. Recommended.

$$$$ Raffles Grand Hotel d'Angkor
1 Charles de Gaulle Blvd, T063-963888, www.raffles.com/siem-reap.
Certainly a magnificent period piece from the outside, Siem Reap's oldest (1930) hotel fails to generate ambience, the rooms are sterile and the design of the huge new wings is uninspired (unforgivable in Angkor). Coupled with this is a history of staff lock-outs and mass sackings that have caused the Raffles brand damage. However, it does have all the mod cons, including sauna, tennis, health and beauty spa, lap pool, gym, 8 restaurants and bars, nightly traditional performances, landscaped gardens, 24-hr valet service and in-house movie channels.

$$$$ Shinta Mani
Junction of Oum Khun and 14th St, T063-761998, www.shintamani.com.
This 18-room luxury, boutique hotel is wonderful in every way: the design, the amenities, the food and the service. The hotel also offers a beautiful pool, library and has mountain bikes available. Provides vocational training to underprivileged youth.

$$$$ Sokha Angkor Resort
Sivatha St, T063-969999, www. sokhahotels.com/siemreap.
One of the few Cambodian-owned 5-star hotels in the country, the rooms and services here are top notch, even if the decor is a little gaudy (if you can't afford to stay here, come and check out the incredibly over-the-top swimming pool, complete with faux temple structures and waterfalls). Also home to an excellent Japanese restaurant. Recommended.

$$$$ Victoria Angkor Hotel
Route 6, T063-760428, www. victoriahotels-asia.com.
Perfection. A beautiful hotel, with that 1930s East-meets-West style that exemplifies the French tradition of *art de vivre*. The superb decor

makes you feel like you are staying in another era. Each room is beautifully decorated with local fabrics and fantastic furniture. Swimming pool, open-air salas, jacuzzi and spa. It's the small touches and attention to detail that stands this hotel apart from the rest. Highly recommended.

$$$$-$$$ FCC Angkor
Near the post office on Pokambor Av, T063-760280, www.fcccambodia.com.
The sister property of the famous **FCC Phnom Penh**, this hotel is set in the grounds of a restored, modernist villa. Rooms offer contemporary luxury and plenty of space but be warned – there is a massive generator at one end of the complex running 24/7 so make sure you are housed well away from here. Also tends to trade more on its reputation so service, food, etc, can be ropey.

$$$$-$$$ Steung Siem Reap Hotel
St 9, T063-965167, www. steungsiemreaphotel.com.
This pleasant rooms in this colonial-style hotel come with cooling wooden floors and many overlook a very quiet pool. There are all the trimmings you'd expect in this price range, including gym, sauna, free Wi-Fi, free breakfast, a/c, huge bathtubs. Service and food average but still a good spot.

$$$$-$$$ Suorkear Villa
Sala Kamroeuk village, T063-764156, www.suorkearvilla.com.
Set in a very peaceful, private garden compound a couple of kilometres east of town, this 17-room/suite 'boutique' resort is unpretentious yet stylish. There's free breakfast, Wi-Fi, a restaurant and complimentary transfers to and from town. The pool is cute as well. All rooms are,

of course, a/c with TV and en suite hot-water facilities. Recommended.

$$$-$$ Casa Angkor
Corner of Chhay St and Oum Khun St, T063-966234, www.casaangkorhotel.com.
This is a good-looking, pleasant and well-managed 21-room hotel. 3 classes of room, all a decent size, well appointed and with cool wooden floors. Friendly reception and efficient staff. Restaurant, beer garden and reading room.

$$$-$$ La Noria
On the road running along the east side of the river, just past the 'stone' bridge, T063-964242, www.lanoriaangkor.com.
Almost perfect riverside setting for this gorgeous small resort. Tranquil gardens, a small pool and a real away-from-it-all vibe seduces guests who stay in brightly coloured a/c and en suite rooms each with their own balcony. No TV, very quiet and decent restaurant. Recommended.

$$$-$$ Molly Malone's
Old Market area, T063-963533, www.mollymalonescambodia.com.
Fantastic rooms with 4-poster beds and good clean bathrooms. Irish pub downstairs. Lovely owners. Recommended.

$$$-$$ Passaggio
Near the Old Market, T063-760324, www.passaggio-hotel.com.
15 double and 2 family rooms, spacious, a/c, minibar and cable TV, internet, laundry service, bar and restaurant, outdoor terrace.

$$$-$$ Soria Moria
Wat Bo Rd, T063-964768, www.thesoriamoria.com.
Excellent, well-run small hotel with a roof-top bar and a decent restaurant. Rooms – all en suite, with contemporary

Asian flourishes, a/c and TVs – are quiet; the upper ones have nice airy views over the town. The enlightened owners have now transferred half the ownership to their Khmer staff as part of an ongoing project to create sustainable, locally owned hotels in the area. Highly recommended.

$$ Borann
On the eastern side of the river, north of NH 6, just behind La Noria, T063-964740, www.borann.com.
This is an attractive hotel in a delightful garden with a pool. It is secluded and private. 5 small buildings each contain 4 comfortable rooms; some have a/c, some fan only.

$$ Mekong Angkor Palace Hotel
21 Sivatha St, T063-963636, www.mekongangkorpalaces.com.
Excellent mid-range, great-value hotel in a good central location. All the spotless rooms are trimmed with a contemporary Khmer vibe, free Wi-Fi, a/c, hot-water bathrooms and TVs. Room rates also include breakfast and there's an excellent pool. Recommended.

$$ Shadow of Angkor II
Wat Bo Rd, T063-760363, www.shadowofangkor.com.
Set on a quiet road this is the sister guesthouse of **Shadow of Angkor I** located on the market side of the river. Also offers well-located, good-value, well-run mid-range accommodation. As well as being clean and comfortable most rooms have balconies and all have a/c, free Wi-Fi, TV and hot water.

$$ The Villa
153 Taphul St, T063-761036, www.thevillasiemreap.com.
From the outside this place looks like a funky little guesthouse but some of the rooms are small and dark. All have a/c, TV and shower while the more expensive deluxe rooms are spacious and spotless.

$$-$ Bopha
On the east side of the river, T063-964928, www.bopha-angkor.com.
Stunning hotel. Good rooms with all the amenities, decorated with local furniture and fabrics. Brilliant Thai-Khmer restaurant. Highly recommended.

$$-$ Home Sweet Home
Wat Bo area, near the royal palace garden, T063-760279, www.homesweethomeangkor.com.
Popular, and a favourite of the moto drivers (who get a kickback). Regardless, it's still got quite good, clean rooms, some with TV and a/c.

$$-$ Jasmine Lodge
Airport Rd near to town centre, T012-784980, www.jasminelodge.com.
One of the best budget deals in town, **Jasmine** is often fully booked, and with good reason. The super-friendly owner Kunn and his family go out of their way to make this a superlative place to stay; there's free Wi-Fi, breakfast can be included in the rate on request, there are huge shared areas for sitting, a book exchange, tour bookings, bus tickets, etc. There is a huge spread of rooms from basic ones with a fan and shared facilities to sparkling new accommodation with a/c, TV and hot-water bathrooms. Highly recommended.

$$-$ Rambutan Resort
Wat Damnak area (past Martini Bar), T012-885366, www.rambutans.info.
Good, clean rooms and decent restaurant.

$$-$ Sala Bai
155 Taphul Rd, T063-963329, www. salabai.com.
Part of an NGO programme that trains disadvantaged young Cambodians to work in the hospitality industry. The rooms are decent enough, in a good location and the suite is an excellent deal. Cheaper rooms have fan, pricier ones a/c, all have private hot-water showers. Gets booked up so reserve in advance. See also Restaurants, below

$$-$ Two Dragons Guesthouse
Wat Bo Village, T012-868551, www. twodragons-asia.com.
Very pleasant, clean rooms. Good little Thai restaurant. The owner, Gordon, is very well informed and runs www. talesofasia.com. He can organize a whole range of exciting tours around the area.

$ Bou Savy
Just outside town off the main airport road, T063-964967, www. bousavyguesthouse.com.
One of the best budget options in town, this tiny and very friendly family-owned guesthouse is set in soothing gardens and offers a range of rooms with fan or a/c. Also offers breakfast, internet and has some nice public areas. Recommended.

$ Earthwalkers
Just off the airport road, T012-967901.
Popular European-run budget guesthouse. Good gardens and pool table. Bit far out of town.

$ Mahogany Guesthouse
Wat Bo St, T063-963417/012-768944, proeun@bigpond.com.kh.
Fan and some a/c. An attractive and popular guesthouse, lovely wooden floor upstairs (try to avoid

staying downstairs), coffee-making facilities and friendly atmosphere.

$ Neth Socheata
10 Thnou St, directly opposite the Old Market, T063-963294, www. nethsocheatahotel.com.
One of the Siem Reap's best deals, this small budget guesthouse, tucked away down a quiet alley opposite the market, has very nice, clean, pleasantly decorated rooms. All have en suite hot-water facilities and either a/c or fan. The best rooms have small balconies while others are windowless. There's free Wi-Fi and a friendly welcome. Recommended.

Restaurants

Near the moat there are a number of cheap food and drink stalls, bookshops and a posse of hawkers selling film, souvenirs, etc. Outside the entrance to Angkor Wat is a larger selection of cafés and restaurants including the sister restaurant to **The Blue Pumpkin** (see page 52), serving good sandwiches and breakfasts, ideal for takeaway.

$$$ Abacus
Route 6 to the airport, turn right at Acleda bank, T063-763660, www. cafeabacus.com.
A little further out from the main Old Market area, this place is considered one of the best restaurants in town. Offering French and Cambodian, everything is fantastic here. The fish is superb, the steak is to die for. Recommended.

$$$ Barrio
Sivatha St, away from the central area, T012-756448.
Fantastic French and Khmer food. A favourite of expats. Recommended.

$$$ Chez Sophea and Matthiu
Outside Angkor Wat, T012-858003.
A great place in the evening serving
Khmer and French cuisine. Romantic
setting. It closes around 2100, but later
if you want to stay for a digestif or 2.

$$$ Le Malraux
Sivatha Bvld, T063-966041, www.le-
malraux-siem-reap.com.
Daily 0700-2400.
Sophisticated French cuisine served
in this excellent restaurant. Also
offers Khmer and Asian dishes,
great wine list and good cognacs.
Patio or indoor seating.

$$$-$$ Sala Bai Restaurant School
See Where to stay. Open for breakfast
and lunch only.
Taking in students from the poorest
areas of Cambodia, **Sala Bai** trains
them in catering skills and places
them in establishments around town.
Service is not the best as students are
quite shy practising their English, but
a little bit of patience will help them
through. Highly recommended.

$$$-$$ Soria Moria Fusion Kitchen
See Where to stay, above. 0700-2200.
Serves a range of local, Scandinavian
and Japanese specialities. Wed
night is popular, when all tapas
dishes and drinks, including
cocktails, cost US$1 each.

$$ The Blue Pumpkin
Old Market area, T063-963574, www.
tbpumpkin.com.
Western and Asian food and
drinks. Sandwiches, ice cream,
pitta, salads and pasta.

$$ Bopha
See Where to stay, above.
Fantastic Thai/Khmer restaurant in

a lovely, tranquil garden setting.
One of the absolute best in
town. Highly recommended.

$$ Butterflies Gardens
Just off Wat Bo Rd, T063-761211,
www.butterfliesofangkor.com.
Daily 0800-2200.
Tropical butterflies flit around a koi-filled
pond in this slightly odd eatery. The
food is Khmer/Asian and is average
but the setting is well worth a visit.

$$ Molly Malone's
See Where to stay, above, T063-963533.
Lovely Irish bar offering classic
dishes such as Irish stew, shepherd's
pie, roasts, and fish and chips.

$$ Red Piano
341 St 8, northwest of the Old Market,
T063-963240, www.redpiano
cambodia.com.
An institution in Siem Reap, based
in a 100-year-old colonial building.
Coffee, sandwiches, salad and
pastas. Cocktail bar offering a range
of tipples, including one dedicated
to Angelina Jolie (who came here
while working on *Tomb Raider*).

$$ Singing Tree Café
Alley West St, Old Market area, T09-263
5500, www.singingtreecafe.com. Tue-Sun
0800-2100.
Brilliant diner/community centre. Tasty
European and Khmer home cooking,
with plenty of veggie options. Also hosts
a DVD library and a fairtrade shop.

$$ Soup Dragon
No 369, St 8, T063-964933.
Serves a variety of Khmer and
Vietnamese dishes but its speciality
is soups in earthenware pots cooked
at the table. Breezy and clean, a

light and colourful location. Upstairs bar, happy hour 1600-1930.

$$ The Sugar Palm
Taphul Rd, T063-964838, www. thesugarpalm.com/spsr. Closed Sun.
Sophisticated Khmer restaurant, with immaculate service and casual ambience.

$$ Tell Steakhouse
374 Sivatha St, T063-963289.
Swiss/German/Austrian restaurant and bar. Branch of the long-established Phnom Penh restaurant. Serves excellent fondue and raclette, imported beer and sausages. Reasonable prices and generous portions.

$$ Viroth's Restaurant
246 Wat Bo St, T012-826346, www.viroth-restaurant.com.
Upmarket place offering very good modern Khmer cuisine plus a few Western staples. Looks more expensive than it actually is, and is good value.

$ Khmer Kitchen
Opposite Old Market and Alley West, T063-964154, www.khmerkitchens.com/siemreap.
Tasty cheap Khmer dishes service can be a little slow, but the food is worth waiting for. Sit on the alley side for good people-watching. Try the pumpkin pie (more of an omelette than a pie).

Bars and clubs

Pub Street may sound a bit brash by name but it has several good bars and restaurants.

Angkor What?
Pub St, T012-490755.
Friendly staff, popular with travellers and young expats.

Fresh at Chilli Si Dang
East River Rd, T017-875129.
Open 0800-late.
Laid-back atmosphere, friendly service away from the tourist drag. Happy hour between 1700 and 2100.

Laundry
Near the Old Market, turn right off 'Pub St', T012-246912. Open till late.
Funky little bar.

Linga
Pub St Alley, T012-246912, www.lingabar.com.
Gay-friendly bar offering a wide selection of cocktails. Great whisky sours.

Miss Wong
The Lane (behind Pub St), T092-428332, www.misswong.net. Open 1700-0100.
Cute little bar serving sharp cocktails in an Old Shanghai setting.

Temple Club
Pub St, T015-999909.
Popular drinking hole, dimly lit, good music. Not related to its seedier namesake in Phnom Penh.

The Warehouse
Opposite Old Market area, T063-964600, www.thewarehousesiemreap.com. Open 1000-0300.
Popular bar, good service and Wi-Fi.

X Rooftop Bar
Sok San Rd, top of Sivataha St (you'll see the luminous X from most high-rise buildings in town), T012-263271, http:// xbar.asia. Open 1600-sunrise.
The latest-closing bar in town. Happy hour 1600-1730.

Zone One
Taphul Village, T012-912347.
Open 1800-late.
The place to experience local nightlife.

Entertainment

Music

A popular Sat evening attraction is the one-man concert put on by **Dr Beat Richner** (Beatocello), founder of the Jayavarman VII hospital for children. Run entirely on voluntary donations the 3 hospitals in the foundation need US$9 million per year in order to treat Cambodian children free of charge. He performs at the hospital, on the road to Angkor, at 1915, 1 hr, free admission but donations gratefully accepted. An interesting and worthwhile experience.

Shadow puppetry

This is one of the finest performing arts of the region. The **Bayon Restaurant**, Wat Bo Rd, has regular shadow puppet shows in the evening. Local NGO, **Krousar Thmey**, often tours its shadow puppet show to Siem Reap. The show is performed by underprivileged children (who have also made the puppets) at **La Noria Restaurant** (Wed 1930 but check as they can be irregular). Donations accepted.

Shopping

Outside Phnom Penh, Siem Reap is about the only place whose markets are worth browsing for genuinely interesting souvenirs. **Old Market** (Psar Chars) is not a large market but stall holders and keepers of the surrounding shops have developed quite a good understanding of what tickles the appetite of foreigners: Buddhist statues and icons, reproductions of Angkor figures, silks, cottons, *kramas*, sarongs, silverware, leather puppets and rice paper rubbings of Angkor bas-reliefs are unusual mementos. In the night market area, off Sivatha St, you'll find bars, spas and cafés. The original night market, towards the back, has more original stalls, but is slightly more expensive.

Boutique Senteurs d'Angkor, opposite Old Market, T063-964801, www.senteursdangkor.com. Sells a good selection of handicrafts, carvings, silverware, silks, handmade paper, cards, scented oils, incense, pepper and spices. **Chantiers Écoles**, Stung Thmey St, down a short lane off Sivatha St, T063-963330. A school for orphaned children that trains them in carving, sewing and weaving. Products are on sale under the name **Les Artisans d'Angkor** and raise 30% of the school's running costs.

What to do

Helicopter and balloon rides

For those wishing to see Angkor from a different perspective it is possible to charter a helicopter. In many ways, it is only from the air that you can really grasp the size and scale of Angkor and a short flight will certainly be a memorable experience. A cheaper alternative for a good aerial view is to organize a balloon ride above the temples. The tethered balloons float 200 m above Angkor Wat for about 10 mins, US$10 per trip. The balloon company is based about 1 km from the main gates from Angkor Wat, on the road from the airport to the temples. **Helicopters Cambodia**, *65 St Hup Quan, near Old Market, T063-963316, www.helicopterscambodia.com.* A New Zealand company offering chartered flights around the temples from US$75 per person.

Therapies

Khmer, Thai, reflexology and Japanese massage are readily available. Many masseuses will come to your hotel.

Frangipani, *24 Hup Guan St, near Angkor Hospital for Children, T063-964391, www.frangipanisiemreap.com.* Professional masseuse offers aromatherapy, reflexology and other treatments.

Mutita Spa, *Borei Angkor Resort and Spa, Route 6, T063-964406.* Offers unique J'Pong therapy, which is a traditional Cambodian heat and relaxation treatment using herbal steam.

Seeing Hands, *324 Sivatha St.* Massage by sight-impaired individuals. US$3 per hr. Highly recommended.

Tour operators

Asia Pacific Travel, *No 100, Route 6, T063-760862, www.angkortravelcambodia.com.* Tours of Angkor and the region.

Buffalo Tours, *556 Tep Vong St, Khum Svay Dangkom, T063-965670, www.buffalotours.com.* Wide range of customized tours.

Exotissimo Travel, *No 300, Route 6, T063-964323, www.exotissimo.com.* Tours of Angkor and sites beyond.

Hidden Cambodia Adventure Tours, *T012-655201, www.hiddencambodia.com.* Specializes in dirt-bike tours to remote areas and off-the-track temple locations. Recommended for the adventurous.

Journeys Within, *on the outskirts of Siem Reap towards the temples, T063-966463, www.journeys-within.com.* Customized tours, visiting temples and experiencing the everyday lives of Cambodians.

Khmer Angkor Tour Guide Association, *on the road to Angkor, T063-964347, www.khmerangkortourguide.com.* The association has well-trained and well-briefed guides; some speak English better than others. The going rate is US$20-25 per day.

Mr Hak, *T012-540336, www.angkortaxidriver.com.* Provides an excellent service offering packages and tours around Angkor and the surrounding area. Recommended.

Terre Cambodge, *Huap Guan St, near Angkor Hospital for Children, T092-476682, www.terrecambodge.com.* Offers tours with a twist, including cruises on an old sampan boat. Not cheap but worth it for the experience.

Two Dragons Guesthouse, *see Where to stay, above.* Can organize off-the-beaten-track tours. Owner Gordon Sharpless is a very knowledgeable and helpful fellow.

WHL Cambodia, *Wat Bo Rd, T063-963854, www.angkorhotels.org.* Locally run website for booking hotels and tours with a responsible tourism approach.

World Express Tours & Travel, *St No 11 (Old Market area), T063-963600, www.worldexpresstour.com.* Can organize tours all over Cambodia. Also books local and international air/bus tickets. A good place to extend visas. Friendly service.

Transport

For information on transport between Siem Reap and Angkor, see page 10.

Airport

Siem Reap Airways and the national carrier **Cambodia Angkor Air** have connections with **Phnom Penh**. Book in advance. All departure taxes are now included in the ticket price.

Siem Reap Airport, 7 km from Siem Reap, T063-963148, is the closest to the

Angkor ruins. A moto into town is US$1, a taxi US$7. Guesthouse owners often meet flights. Visas can be issued upon arrival US$20 (฿1000), photo required.

Bicycle
The **White Bicycles** scheme, www. thewhitebicycles.org, set up by Norwegian expats (see page 10). Recommended. **Khemara**, opposite the Old Market, T063-964512, rents bicycles for US$2 per day.

Boat
The ferry docks are at Chong Khneas, 15 km south of Siem Reap on the Tonlé Sap Lake, near Phnom Krom. Taxis, tuk-tuks and motodops wait at the dock; a motodop into town will cost US$2. Tickets and enquiries, T012-581358. To **Phnom Penh**, US$35, 5-6 hrs. It is a less appealing option in the dry season when low water levels necessitate transfers to small, shallow draft vessels. In case of extremely low water levels a bus or pickup will need to be taken for part of the trip. The mudbank causeway between the lake and the outskirts of Siem Reap is hard to negotiate and some walking may be necessary (it's 12 km from Siem Reap to Bindonville harbour). Boats depart Siem Reap at 0700 from Chong Khneas about 12 km away on the Tonlé Sap Lake (a motodop will cost US$2 to get here) arriving in Phnom Penh Port at Sisowath Quay (end of 106 St). Tickets and enquiries, T012-581358.

Bus
Different companies use different bus stations. The Chong Kov Sou station is 7 km west of Siem Reap. Motodops into town cost US$1.50-2, tuk-tuks US$3. Others arrive near the Old Market.

A/c buses are one of the most convenient and comfortable ways to travel from Siem Reap to **Phnom Penh**, US$6-13, 6 hrs. At the time of going to press the road between Siem Reap and Phnom Penh was undergoing a massive redevelopment and consequently parts of it have been reduced to a rutted, dirt-track. Until it is completed expect increased journey times. Almost every guesthouse or hotel sells tickets although it is easy enough to pick up from the bus stations/terminal. In peak periods, particularly Khmer New Year, it is important to purchase tickets a day or 2 prior to travel. **Neak Krorhorm Travel**, **GST**, **Mekong Express** and **Capitol** depart Siem Reap (from near the Old Market) between 0630 and 0800, and the same from Phnom Penh bus station.

Taxi
A shared taxi to **Phnom Penh** will cost US$10.

Background
Cambodia

History

Rise of the Lunar and Solar dynasties

For thousands of years Indochina was isolated from the rest of the world and was virtually unaffected by the rise and fall of the early Chinese dynasties. India and China 'discovered' Southeast Asia early in the first millennium AD and trade networks were quickly established. The Indian influence was particularly strong in the Mekong basin area. The Khmers adopted and adapted Indian script as well as their ideas about astrology, religion (Buddhism and Hinduism) and royalty (the cult of the semi-divine ruler). Today, several other aspects of Cambodian culture are recognizably Indian in origin – including classical literature and dance. Religious architecture also followed Indian models. These Indian cultural influences which took root in Indochina gave rise to a legend to which Cambodia traces its historical origins. An Indian Brahmin called Kaundinya, travelling in the Mekong Delta area, married Soma, daughter of the Naga (the serpent deity), or Lord of the Soil. Their union, which founded the 'Lunar Dynasty' of Funan (a pre-Angkorian Kingdom), symbolized the fertility of the kingdom and occupies a central place in Khmer cosmology. The Naga, Soma's father, helpfully drank the floodwaters of the Mekong, enabling people to cultivate the land.

Funan

The kingdom of Funan – the forerunner of Kambuja – was established on the Mekong by tribal people from South China in the middle of the third century AD and became the earliest Hindu state in Southeast Asia. Funan was known for its elaborate irrigation canals which controlled the Mekong floodwaters, irrigated the paddy fields and prevented the incursion of seawater. By the fifth century Funan had extended its influence over most of present day Cambodia, as well as Indochina and parts of the Malay peninsula. Leadership was measured by success in battle and the ability to provide protection, and in recognition of this fact, rulers from the Funan period onward incorporated the suffix 'varman' (meaning protection) into their names. Records of a third century Chinese embassy give an idea of what it was like: "There are walled villages, places and dwellings. The men ... go about naked and barefoot. ... Taxes are paid in gold, silver and perfume. There are books and libraries and they can use the alphabet." Twentieth-century excavations suggest a seafaring people engaged in extensive trade with both India and China, and elsewhere.

Chenla

The 'Solar Dynasty' of Chenla was a vassal kingdom of Funan, probably first based on the Mekong at the junction with the Mun tributary, but it rapidly grew in power, and was centred in the area of present day southern Laos. It was the immediate predecessor of Kambuja and the great Khmer Empire. According to Khmer legend, the kingdom was the result of the marriage of Kambu, an ascetic, to a celestial nymph named Mera. The people of Chenla – the Kambuja, or the sons of Kambu – lent their name to the country. In AD 540 a Funan prince married a Chenla princess, uniting the Solar and Lunar dynasties. The prince sided with his wife and Funan was swallowed by Chenla. The first capital of this fusion was at **Sambor**. King Ishanavarman (AD 616-635) established a new capital at Sambor Prei Kuk, 30 km from modern Kompong Thom, in the centre of the country (the monuments of which are some of the best preserved of this period). His successor, Jayavarman I, moved the capital to the region of Angkor Borei near Takeo.

Quarrels in the ruling family led to the break-up of the state later in the seventh century: it was divided into 'Land Chenla', a farming culture located north of the Tonlé Sap (maybe centred around Champassak in Laos), and 'Water Chenla', a trading culture based along the Mekong. Towards the end of the eighth century Water Chenla became a vassal of Java's powerful Sailendra Dynasty and members of Chenla's ruling family were taken back to the Sailendra court. This period, from the fall of Funan until the eighth century, is known as the pre-Angkorian period and is a somewhat hazy time in the history of Cambodia. The Khmers remained firmly under Javanese suzerainty until Jayavarman II (AD 802-850), who was born in central Java, returned to the land of his ancestors around AD 800 to change the course of Cambodian history.

Angkor and the god-kings

Jayavarman II, the Khmer prince who had spent most of his life at the Sailendra court, claimed independence from Java and founded the Angkor Kingdom to the north of the Tonlé Sap in AD 802, at about the same time as Charlemagne became Holy Roman Emperor in Europe. They were men cast in the same mould, for both were empire builders. His far-reaching conquests at Wat Phou (Laos) and Sambhupura (Sambor) won him immediate political popularity on his return and he became king in AD 790. In AD 802 he declared himself a World Emperor and to consolidate and legitimize his position he arranged his for coronation by a Brahmin priest, declaring himself the first Khmer devaraja, or god-king, a tradition continued today. From then on, the reigning monarch was identified with Siva, the king of the Hindu gods. In the centuries that followed, successive devaraja strove to outdo their predecessors by building bigger and finer temples to house the royal linga, a phallic symbol which is the symbol of Siva and the devaraja. The god-kings commanded the absolute allegiance of their subjects, giving them control of a vast pool of labour which was used to build an advanced and prosperous agricultural civilization. For many years historians and archaeologists maintained that the key to this agricultural wealth lay in a sophisticated hydraulic – that is irrigated – system of agriculture which allowed the Khmers to produce up to three harvests a year. However, this view of Angkorian agriculture has come under increasing scrutiny in recent years and now there are many who believe that flood-retreat – rather than irrigated – agriculture was the key. Jayavarman II installed himself in successive capitals north of the Tonlé Sap, secure from attack by the Sailendras, and he ruled until AD 850, when he died on the banks of the Great Lake at the original capital, Hariharalaya, in the Roluos area (Angkor).

Jayavarman III (AD 850-877) continued his father's traditions and ruled for the next 27 years. He expanded his father's empire at Hariharalaya and was the original founder of the laterite temple at Bakong. **Indravarman** (AD 877-889), his successor, was the first of the great temple-builders of Angkor and somewhat overshadowed the work of Jayavarman III. His means to succession are somewhat ambiguous but it is generally agreed that he overthrew Jayavarman III violently. Unlike his predecessor, Indravarman was not the son of a king but more than likely the nephew of Jayavarman's II Queen. He expanded and renovated the capital, building Preah Ko Temple and developing Bakong. Indravarman is considered one of the key players in Khmer history. Referred to as the "lion among kings" and "prince endowed with all the merits", his architectural projects established precedents that were emulated by those that followed him. After Indravarman's death his sons fought for the King's title. The victor, at the end of the ninth century was **Yasovarman I** (AD 889-900). The battle is believed to have destroyed the palace, thus spurring a move to Angkor. He called his new capital Yasodharapura and copied the water system his father had devised at Roluos on an even larger scale, using the waters of the Tonlé Sap. After Yasovarman's death in AD 900 his son **Harshavarman** (AD 900-923) took the throne, until he died 23 years later. Harshavarman was well regarded, one particular inscription saying that he "caused the joy of the universe". Upon his death, his brother **Ishanarvarman II**, assumed the regal status. In AD 928, **Jayavarman IV** set up a rival capital about 65 km from Angkor at Koh Ker and ruled for the next 20 years. After Jayavarman IV's death there was a period of upheaval as **Harsharvarman II** tried unsuccessfully to lead the empire. **Rajendravarman** (AD 944-968), Jayarvarman's nephew, managed to take control of the empire and moved the court back to Angkor, where the Khmer kings remained. He chose to build outside of the former capital Bakheng, opting instead for the region south of the East Baray. Many saw him as the saviour of Angkor with one inscription reading: "He restored the holy city of Yashodharapura, long deserted, and rendered it superb and charming." Rajendravarman orchestrated a campaign of solidarity – bringing together a number of provinces and claiming back territory, previously under Yasovarman I. From the restored capital he led a successful crusade against the Champa in what is now Vietnam. A devout Buddhist, he erected some of the first Buddhist temples in the precinct. Upon Rajendravarman's death, his son **Jayavarman V** (AD 968-

1001), still only a child, took the royal reigns. Once again the administrative centre was moved, this time to the west, where Ta Keo was built. The capital was renamed Jayendranagari. Like his father, Jayavarman V was Buddhist but was extremely tolerant of other religions. At the start of his tenure he had a few clashes with local dissidents but things settled down and he enjoyed relative peace during his rule. The next king, **Udayadityavarman I**, lasted a few months before being ousted. For the next few years Suryavarman I and Jayaviravarman battled for the King's title.

The formidable warrior **King Suryavarman I** (1002-1049) won. He may originally have come from the Malay peninsula. He was a determined leader and made all of his officials swear a blood oath of allegiance. He undertook a series of military campaigns geared towards claiming Mon territory in central and southern Thailand and victoriously extended the Khmer empire into Lower Menam, as well as into Laos and established a Khmer capital in Louvo (modern day Lopburi in Thailand). Suryavarman holds the record for the greatest territorial expansion ever achieved in the Khmer Empire. The Royal Palace (Angkor Thom), the West Baray and the Phimeanakas pyramid temples were Suryavarman's main contributions to Angkor's architectural heritage (see pages 27 and 64). He continued the royal Hindu cult but also tolerated Mahayana Buddhism.

On Suryavarman's death, the Khmer Kingdom began to fragment. His three successors had short, troubled reigns and the Champa kingdom captured, sacked and razed the capital. When the king's son, **Udayadityavarman II** (1050-1066), assumed the throne, havoc ensued as citizens revolted against him and some of his royal appointments.

When Udayadityavarman II died, his younger brother, **Harsharvarman III** (1066-1080), last in the line of the dynasty, stepped in. During his reign, there were reports of discord and further defeat at the hands of the Cham.

In 1080 a new kingdom was founded by a northern provincial governor claiming aristocratic descent. He called himself **Jayavarman VI** (1080-1107) and is believed to have led a revolt against the former king. He never settled at Angkor, living instead in the northern part of the kingdom. He left monuments at Wat Phou in southern Laos and Phimai, in Thailand. There was an intermittent period where Jayavarman's IV brother, **Dharanindravarman** (1107-1112) took the throne but he was overthrown by his grand-nephew **Suryavarman II** (1113-1150), who soon became the greatest leader the Angkor Empire had ever seen. He worked prolifically on a broad range of projects and achieved some of most impressive architectural feats and political manoeuvres seen within the Angkorian period. He resumed diplomatic relations with China, the Middle Kingdom, and was held in the greatest regard by the then Chinese Emperor. He expanded the Khmer Empire as far as Lopburi, Siam, Pagan in Myanmar, parts of Laos and into the Malay peninsula. He attacked the Champa state relentlessly, particularly Dai Vet in Northern Vietnam, eventually defeating them in 1144-1145, and capturing and sacking the royal capital, Vijaya. He left an incredible, monumental legacy behind, being responsible for the construction of Angkor Wat, an architectural masterpiece that represented the height of the Khmer's artistic genius, Phnom Rung temple (Khorat) and Banteay Samre. A network of roads was built to connect regional capitals.

However, his success was not without its costs – his widespread construction put serious pressure on the general running of the kingdom and major reservoirs silted up during this time; there was also an intensified discord in the provinces and his persistent battling fuelled an ongoing duel between the Cham and Khmers that was to continue (and eventually be avenged) long after his death.

Suryavarman II deposed the King of Champa in 1145 but the Cham regained their independence in 1149 and the following year, Suryavarman died after a disastrous attempt to conquer Annam (northern Vietnam). The throne was usurped by **Tribhuvanadityavarman** in 1165, who died in 1177, when the Cham seized their chance of revenge and sacked Angkor in a surprise naval attack. This was the Khmer's worst recorded defeat – the city was completely annihilated. The 50-year-old **Jayavarman VII** – a cousin of Suryavarman – turned out to be their saviour. He battled the Cham for the next four years, driving them out of the Kingdom. In 1181 he was declared king and seriously hit back, attacking the Chams and seizing their capital, Vijaya. He expanded the Khmer Kingdom further than ever before; its suzerainty stretched from the Malay peninsula in the south to the borders of Burma in the west and the Annamite chain to the northeast.

Jayavarman's VII's first task was to plan a strong, spacious new capital – Angkor Thom; but while that work was being undertaken he set up a smaller, temporary seat of government where he and his court could live in the meantime – Preah Khan meaning 'Fortunate City of Victory'. He also built 102 hospitals throughout his kingdom, as well as a network of roads, along which he constructed resthouses. But because they were built of wood, none of these secular structures survive; only the foundations of four larger ones have been unearthed at Angkor.

Khmer Empire

Under Jayavarman VII (1181-1218) the complex stretched more than 25 km east to west and nearly 10 km north to south, approximately the same size as Manhattan. For five centuries (ninth-13th), the court of Angkor held sway over a vast territory. At its height Khmer influence spanned half of Southeast Asia, from Burma to the southernmost tip of Indochina and from the borders of Yunnan to the Malay Peninsula. The only threat to this great empire was a river-borne invasion in 1177, when the Cham used a Chinese navigator to pilot their canoes up the Mekong. Scenes are depicted in bas-reliefs of the Bayon temple.

Angkor's decline

As was the case duuring Suryavarman II's reign, Jayavarman VII's extensive building campaign put a large amount of pressure on the kingdom's resources and rice was in short supply as labour was diverted into construction.

Jayavarman VII died in 1218 and the Kambujan Empire fell into progressive decline over the next two centuries. Territorially, it was eroded by the eastern migration of the Siamese. The Khmers were unable to prevent this gradual incursion but the diversion of labour to the military rice farming helped seal the fate of Angkor. Another reason for the decline was the introduction of Theravada Buddhism in the 13th century, which undermined the prestige of the king and the priests. There is even a view that climatic change disrupted the agricultural

BARAYS AND THE JAYAVARMAN CONUNDRUM
The case *for* irrigation

By founding his capital at Roluos, just southeast of Angkor, in the middle of an arid plain annually plagued by drought and flash floods, Jayavarman II bequeathed to scholars a geo-climatic conundrum: what possessed him to site the nerve centre of Khmer civilization at such an environmentally unfriendly spot and how did the great city sustain itself through the centuries?

Archaeologists have postulated that the Khmers engineered a complex irrigation system to grow enough rice to feed the city's population. In this view, Angkor was a classic hydraulic society.

In *The Art of Southeast Asia*, Philip Rawson wrote: "Angkor was a capital filled with temples and supporting many inhabitants. But its nucleus was a splendid irrigation project based on a number of huge artificial reservoirs fed by the local rivers and linked to each other by means of a rectangular grid system of canals." The barays, or man-made lakes, fed an intricate network of irrigation channels. The first baray was Lolei, built by Indravarman at the city of Roluos. "The engineering involved at Angkor," Rawson said, "… was vaster and far more sophisticated than anything seen before in that part of the world." Lolei was more than 3.5 km long and 800 m wide. The East Baray was twice the size of Lolei and the West Baray, built during Udayadityavarman II's reign, is thought to have held about four million cubic metres of water when full.

The barays were constructed by building dykes above the level of the land and waiting for the monsoon flood. Because the resultant reservoirs were higher than the surrounding land, there was no need to pump the water to flood the paddy fields: a gap was simply cut in the dyke. The water stored in the barays would have been replenished by each monsoon, making it possible to irrigate the ricelands. With their land being watered year round, the Khmers would be able to grow three crops of rice a year.

The barays were central to the health and vigour of Khmer civilization but because they were sitting targets for enemy saboteurs, they may also have played a part in its downfall. During successive Siamese invasions the irrigation system would have been irreparably damaged and essential maintenance neglected through lack of manpower. The precarious, and artificial, balance of man and nature was disturbed and the irrigation channels cracked and dried up along with the mighty Khmer Empire.

Why Angkor should have gone into decline from about the 13th century has exercised the minds of historians for years. Apart from the destruction of the fragile irrigation system, several other explanations as to Angkor's downfall have been suggested: climatic change, the shift of trade from land to sea-based empires and the corruption of a system which, like the Roman emperors, made the king a demi-god. Some think the builder King Jayavarman VII bankrupted the empire with his vast and ambitious building schemes.

BARAYS AND THE JAYAVARMAN CONUNDRUM
The case *against* irrigation

When the first Westerners stumbled upon the Khmer ruins at Angkor – the lost city in the jungle – in the middle of the 19th century, they judged it to be the finest example of a civilization based upon the massive control of water for irrigation. The sheer size of the monuments, the vast barays storing millions of gallons of water, all seemed to lend force to the notion that here was the finest example of state-controlled irrigation. In Karl Marx's words, the Khmer Kingdom was a society based upon the Asiatic mode of production. The upshot of this was that, by necessity, there needed to be a centralized state and an all-powerful king – leading, in Professor Karl Wittfogel's famous phrase, to a system of 'Oriental Despotism'. Such a view seemed hard to refute – how could such enormous expanses of water in the baray be used for anything but irrigation?

However, in the past decade, archaeologists, irrigation engineers and geographers have challenged the view of the Khmer Kingdom as the hydraulic civilization par excellence. Their challenge rests on four main pillars of evidence. First, they point out that if irrigation was so central to life in Angkor, why is it not mentioned once in over 1000 inscriptions? Second, they question the usual interpretation of Angkorian agriculture contained in the Chinese emissary Chou Ta-kuan's account, *Notes on the customs of Cambodia*, written in 1312. This account talks of "three or four rice harvests a year" – which scholars have assumed means irrigated rice agriculture. However, the detractors put a different interpretation on Chou Ta-kuan's words, arguing that they in fact describe a system of flood retreat agriculture in which rice was sown as the waters of the Great Lake, the Tonlé Sap, receded at the end of the rainy season. Third, they note that aerial photographs show none of the feeder canals needed to carry water from the barays to the fields nor any of the other irrigation structures needed to control water.

Finally, the sceptics draw upon engineering evidence to support their case. They have calculated that the combined storage capacity of all the barays and reservoirs is sufficient to irrigate only 400 ha of riceland – hardly the stuff on which great civilizations are built.

The geographer Philip Stott maintains that flood retreat agriculture would have produced the surplus needed to feed the soldiers, priests and the court of the Khmer god-king, while postulating that the barays were only for urban use. He writes that they were "just like the temple mountains, essentially a part of the urban scene, providing urban symbolism, beauty, water for bathing and drinking, a means of transport, and perhaps a supply of fish as well. Yet, not one drop of their water is likely to have fed the rice fields of Angkor."

The East Baray is now dry but the West Baray is used for fish cultivation.

system and led to Kambuja's demise. After Jayavarman VII, no king seems to have been able to unify the kingdom by force of arms or personality – internal dissent increased while the king's extravagance continued to place a crippling burden on state funds. With its temples decaying and its once-magnificent agricultural system in ruins, Angkor became virtually uninhabitable. In 1431 the royal capital was finally abandoned to the Siamese, who drove the Khmers out and made Cambodia a vassal of the Thai Sukhothai Kingdom.

Explaining Angkor's decline

Why the Angkorian Empire should have declined has always fascinated scholars in the West – in the same way that the decline and fall of the Roman Empire has done. Numerous explanations have been offered, and still the debate remains unresolved. As Anthony Barnett argued in a paper in the *New Left Review* in 1990, perhaps the question should be "Why did Angkor last so long? Inauspiciously sited, it was nonetheless a tropical imperium of 500 years' duration."

There are essentially five lines of argument in the 'Why did Angkor fall?' debate. First, it has been argued that the building programmes became simply so arduous and demanding of ordinary people that they voted with their feet and moved out, depriving Angkor of the population necessary to support a great empire. Second, some scholars present an environmental argument: the great irrigation works silted-up, undermining the empire's agricultural wealth. (This line of argument conflicts with recent work that maintains that Angkor's wealth was never based on hydraulic – or irrigated – agriculture, see pages 64 and 65.) Third, there are those who say that military defeat was the cause – but this only begs the question: why were they defeated in the first place? Fourth, historians with a rather wider view, have offered the opinion that the centres of economic activity in Southeast Asia moved from land-based to sea-based foci, and that Angkor was poorly located to adapt to this shift in patterns of trade, wealth and, hence, power. Lastly, some scholars argue that the religion which demanded such labour of Angkor's subjects became so corrupt that it ultimately corroded the empire from within.

The French at Angkor

Thai ascendency and eventual occupation of Angkor in 1431, led to the city's abandonment and the subsequent invasion of the jungle. Four centuries later, in 1860, Henri Mouhot – a French naturalist – stumbled across the forgotten city, its temple towers enmeshed in the forest canopy. Locals told him they were the work of a race of giant gods. Only the stone temples remained; all the wooden secular buildings had decomposed in the intervening centuries. In 1873 French archaeologist Louis Delaporte removed many of Angkor's finest statues for 'the cultural enrichment of France'. In 1898, the École Française d'Extrême Orient started clearing the jungle, restoring the temples, mapping the complex and making an inventory of the site. Delaporte was later to write the two-volume *Les Monuments du Cambodge*, the most comprehensive Angkorian inventory of its time, and his earlier sketches, plans and reconstructions, published in *Voyage au Cambodge* in 1880 are without parallel.

Culture

The Khmer language

The Khmer language belongs to the Mon-Khmer family, enriched by the Indian Pali and Sanskrit languages and peppered with Thai and French influences. The use of Sanskrit in royal texts became more widespread after the introduction of Mahayana Buddhism in the 12th century (although there are inscriptions dating from the sixth century) and the Pali language spread into Cambodia via Siam with Theravada Buddhism. Khmer is related to languages spoken by hill tribe people of Laos, Vietnam and even Malaysia – but is very different to Thai or Lao. Khmer has no tones, no tenses, and words are attached to the masculine or feminine genders. But Khmer does have 23 vowel-sounds and 33 consonants; it is also a very specific language – for instance, there are 100 different words for types of rice. The Khmer language is written from left to right often with no separation between words.

French was widely spoken by the intelligentsia before 1975 and is still spoken by a few elderly Cambodians. But these days most people seem to want to learn English, and there are informal pavement English schools setting up on Phnom Penh's streets. This has led to some Franco-Anglophone friction. Understandably, the French government – one of Cambodia's largest aid donors – would like to see the French language sustained, perhaps even developed. In 1995 this led to the strange spectacle of language riots on the campus of Phnom Penh's Cambodian University of Technology as students burnt French text books in protest at being forced to learn a language which, they said, "got them nowhere".

Cambodian literature

Religious literature comprises works of religious instruction, derived from the Sanskrit and Pali texts of the Theravada Buddhist canon, the Tripitaka. The Jataka tales are well known in Cambodia and several modern adaptations have been made from these texts. The Jatakas recount the former lives of the historic Buddha and were probably first introduced to Cambodia from Laos. Most of the stories tell of how the Buddha – then a prince – managed to overcome some defect by the use of magic or the assistance of some god, enabling him to be born higher up the scale of birth and re-birth on his long road to nirvana.

The two Khmer epics are the poem of Angkor Wat and the Reamker (or Ramakerti), derived from the Indian Ramayana. Traditionally the literature was recorded by incising palm leaf manuscripts with a sharp stylus, the incisions then being blackened to make them easily visible. From around the 17th century, chap poetry, an import from Thailand, became popular. The poetry took root in monasteries as a means by which monks could more easily teach the laity the lessons of the Buddhist texts. However, over time, they also took on a secular guise and became a means by which more everyday homilies were communicated.

Most of the early literature has been destroyed but there are surviving Sanskrit inscriptions on stone monuments dating from the sixth century and some early palm leaf manuscripts. Many of these are contained in the Bibliothèque Nationale in Paris – the Khmer Rouge managed to destroy most of those housed in monasteries and museums in Cambodia itself.

Historical literature consists largely of inscriptions from Angkor Wat as well as the Cambodian royal chronicles. Fictional literature is diverse in Cambodia and includes the Ipaen folk stories written in prose. French literature has had a profound influence on modern Cambodian literature. The first modern Cambodian novel was Sophat published in 1938. It, and the novels and short stories that followed it, represented a break with the past. The authors wrote of ordinary people, used natural conversation, and wrote in prose. Most of the recent Cambodian novels have been written by Cambodians living abroad – most writers and journalists were either killed by the Khmer Rouge or fled the country.

Arts and architecture

Indian origins

The art of modern Cambodia is almost completely overshadowed by its past. The influence of the Khmers at the height of the empire spread as far as the Malay peninsula in the south, to the Burmese border in the west and the Vietnamese frontier in the north and east. But ancient Khmer culture was itself inherited. Indian influence was particularly strong in the Mekong basin area and the Khmers accepted Indian ideas about astrology, religion and royalty – including the cult of the god-king (*devaraja*). Other elements of Cambodian culture which are recognizably Indian in origin include classical literature and dance, as well as religious architecture. Hindu deities inspired the iconography in much of Cambodian art and Sanskrit gave the Khmers access to a whole new world of ideas. Cambodian influence is very strong in Thai culture as Siam's capture of a large part of the Khmer Empire in the 15th century resulted in many of Cambodia's best scholars, artists and craftsmen being transported to Siam (Thailand).

Artistic revival

The richness of their culture remains a great source of pride for the Khmer people and in the past it has helped forge a sense of national identity. There has been an artistic revival since 1979 and the government has devoted resources to the restoration of monuments and pagodas. (Many local wats have been repaired by local subscription; it is estimated that one-fifth of rural disposable income is given to the upkeep of wats.) The resurgence of Buddhism has been paralleled in recent years by a revival of traditional Khmer culture, which was actively undermined during the Pol Pot years. Today Phnom Penh's two Fine Arts Schools are flourishing again; one teaches music and dance, the other specializes in architecture and archaeology. There is a surprisingly good collection of artefacts in the National

Museum of Arts even though huge quantities of treasure and antiques have been stolen and much of the remainder destroyed by the Khmer Rouge.

Angkor period

The Angkor period (ninth-13th centuries) encapsulated the greatest and best of Cambodia's art and architecture. Much of it shows strong Indian influence. The so-called 'Indianization' of Cambodia was more a product of trade than Hindu proselytism; there was no attempt made at formal conquest, and no great emigration of Indians to the region. In order to meet the Romans' demand for exotic oriental merchandise and commodities, Indian traders ventured into the South China Sea, well before the first century AD when it was discovered that monsoon winds could carry them to the Malay Peninsula and on to Indochina and Cambodia. Because of their reliance on seasonal winds, Indian navigators were obliged to while away many months in countries with which they traded and the influence of their sophisticated culture spread.

But although Khmer art and architecture was rooted in Indian prototypes, the expression and content was distinctively Cambodian. Most of the art from the Angkor period is Hindu although Mahayana Buddhism took hold in the late 12th century. Some Buddhist figures have been dated to as early as the sixth century – the standing Buddhas were carved in the same style as the Hindu deities, minus the sensuous voluptuousness.

The ancient kingdoms of Funan (the Chinese name for the mercantile state encompassing the area southwest of the Mekong Delta, in what is now southern Vietnam and southern Cambodia. First century AD 613) and Chenla (a mountain kingdom centred on northern Cambodia and southern Laos, AD 550-eighth century) were the first to be artistically and culturally influenced by India. In The Art of Southeast Asia Philip Rawson wrote that the art styles of Funan and Chenla were "the greatest phase of pre-Angkor Khmer art, and... we can treat the evolution under these two kingdoms together as a stylistic unity. It was the foundation of classic Khmer art, just as archaic Greek sculpture was the foundation of later classical Greek art".

The Angkor region was strategically important to the Funan Empire as it helped control the trade routes around the region – specifically the Malay Peninsula and the Mekong Delta. The only traces of the kingdom of Funan – whose influence is thought to have spread as far afield as southern Burma and Indonesia – are limited to four Sanskrit inscriptions on stelae and a few sculptures. The earliest surviving Funanese statues were found at Angkor Borei and have been dated to the sixth century. Most represent the Hindu god, Vishnu (patron of King Rudravarman), and their faces are distinctly Angkorian. Scattered remains of these pre-Angkorian periods are all over southern Cambodia – especially between the Mekong and the Tonlé Sap. Most of the earliest buildings would have been made of wood rotted away – there being a paucity of stone in the delta region.

The kingdom of Chenla, based at Sambor and later at Sambor Prei Kuk, expanded at the expense of Funan, which gradually became a vassal state. In the sixth century evidence of a new Chenla Kingdom started to appear in local inscriptions. Chenla inherited Funan's Indianized art and architectural traditions. Some buildings were built of brick and stone and typical architectural relics are brick towers with a square (or sometimes octagonal) plan: a shrine set atop a pedestal comprising of mounting tiers of decreasing size – a style which may have been structurally patterned on early Pallava temples in southeast India. The sculptural work was strongly rooted in Indian ideas but carved in a unique style – many of the statues from this era are in the museum at Phnom Penh. Rawson wrote: "Among the few great stone icons which have survived are some of the world's outstanding masterpieces, while the smaller bronzes reflect the same sophisticated and profound style."

In the late eighth century the Chenla Kingdom collapsed and contact with India came to an end. Chenla is thought to have been eclipsed by the increasingly important Sumatran-based Srivijayan Empire. Jayavarman II, who had lived most of his life in the Sailendra court in Java but who was of royal lineage, returned to Cambodia in about AD 790. Jayavarman II's reign marked the transition period between pre-Angkorian and Angkorian styles – by the ninth century the larger images were recognizably Khmer in style. From Jayavarman II onwards, the kings of Cambodia were regarded as god-kings – or *devaraja* (see page 60).

Jayavarman II established a royal Siva-lingam (phallic) cult which was to prove the inspiration for successive generations of Khmer kings. "He summoned a Brahmin learned in the appropriate texts, and erected a lingam... with all the correct Indian ritual," Rawson said. "This lingam, in which the king's own soul was held to reside, became the source and centre of power for the Khmer Dynasty. At the same time – and by that act – he severed all ties of dependence upon Indonesia." To house the sacred lingam each king in turn built a new temple, some of the mightiest and finest of the monuments of the Khmer civilization.

Angkor temples

The temples at Angkor were modelled on those of the kingdom of Chenla, which in turn were modelled on Indian temples. They represent Mount Meru – the home of the gods of Indian cosmology. The central towers symbolize the peaks of Mount Meru, surrounded by a wall which represents the earth. The moats and basins represent the oceans. The devaraja was enshrined in the centre of the religious complex, which acted as the spiritual axis of the kingdom. The people believed their apotheosized king communicated directly with the gods.

The central tower sanctuaries housed the images of the Hindu gods to whom the temples were dedicated. Dead members of the royal and priestly families were accorded a status on a par with these gods. Libraries to store the sacred scriptures were also built within the ceremonial centre. The temples were mainly built to shelter the images of the gods. Unlike Christian churches, Muslim mosques and some Buddhist pagodas, they were not intended to accommodate worshippers. Only priests, the servants of the god, were allowed into the interiors. The 'congregation' would mill around outside in open courtyards or wooden pavilions. The first temples were of a very simple design but with time they became more grandiose and doors and galleries were added. Most of

Angkor's buildings are made from a soft sandstone which is easy to work. It was transported to the site from Phnom Kulen, about 30 km to the northeast. Laterite was used for foundations, core material and enclosure walls as it was widely available and could be easily cut into blocks. The Khmer sandstone architecture has echoes of earlier wooden structures: gallery roofs are sculpted with false tiles, while balustred windows imitate wooden ones. A common feature of Khmer temples was false doors and windows on the sides and backs of sanctuaries and other buildings. In most cases there was no need for well-lit rooms and corridors as hardly anyone ever went into them. That said, the galleries round the central towers in later temples, such as Angkor Wat, indicate that worshippers did use the temples for ceremonial circumambulation when they would contemplate the inspiring bas-reliefs from the Ramayana and Mahabharata.

In Europe and the Middle East the arch and vault were used in contemporary buildings but at Angkor architects used the false vault – also known as corbelling. It is strange that, despite the architectural innovation of the Khmer, the principle of the arch, used to such great effect in Christian and Muslim architecture, should have eluded them. Corbelling is a fairly primitive vaulting system so the interiors of sanctuaries could never be very large. The stones were often laid without staggering the vertical joints and mortar was not used. The builders relied on the weight of the structure, gravity and a good fit between the stones to hold their buildings together. This is why so many of the temples have collapsed.

Despite the court's conversion to Mahayana Buddhism in the 12th century (under Jayavarman VII) the architectural ground-plans of temples did not alter much – even though they were based on Hindu cosmology. The idea of the god-king was simply grafted onto the new state religion and statues of the Buddha rather than the gods of the Hindu pantheon were used to represent the god-king (see page 60). One particular image of the Buddha predominated at Angkor in which he wears an Angkor-style crown, with a conical top which is encrusted with jewellery.

There are some scholars who maintain that Angkor has, perhaps, been over praised. Anthony Barnett in the *New Left Review* in 1990, for example, wrote: "...to measure [Angkor's] greatness by the fact that it is nearly a mile square is to deny it a proper admiration through hyperbole. Thus the Church of Saint Sophia, to take one example, was for nearly a millennium the largest domed space in the world until St Peter's was constructed. Saint Sophia still stands in Istanbul. It was built 600 years before Angkor Wat, while Khmer architects never managed to discover the principles of the arch".

Sculpture

The sculpture of the early temples at Angkor is rather stiff and plain, but forms the basis for the ornate bas-reliefs of the later Angkor Wat. Lintel-carving became a highly developed art form at an early stage in the evolution of Khmer architecture. (The lintel is a horizontal supporting stone at the top of a window or door opening.) The use of columns around doorways was another distinctive feature – they too had their antecedents in the earlier Chenla period. Frontons – the masonry covering originally used to conceal the corbelled end gables – were elaborate at Angkor. They were intricately carved and conveyed stories from the *Ramayana* and other great Hindu epics. The carved fronton is still used in temples throughout modern Thailand, Laos and Cambodia. Sanctuary doorways, through which priests would pass to enter the sacred heart of the temple, were an important site for icons. Ornately carved sandstone blocks were placed in front of and above the true lintel.

Angkor's most impressive carvings are its bas-reliefs which, like the fronton, were devoted to allegorical depictions and mostly illustrate stories from the Hindu classics, the *Mahabharata* and *Ramayana*. The latter is best exemplified at the Baphuon (11th century) – see page 27. Details of the everyday lives of the Angkor civilization can be pieced together thanks to these bas-reliefs. Those on the Bayon illustrate the weaponry and armour used in battle, market scenes, fishing and cockfighting – probably the Khmers' favourite excuse for gambling. In contrast to the highly sculpted outer walls of the temples, the interiors were typically bare; this has led to speculation that they may originally have been decorated with murals.

Laterite, which is a coarse soft stone, found widely across Southeast Asia, was excavated to form many of the moats and barays at Angkor. Early structures such as those at Preah Ko in the Roluos group were built in brick. The brickwork was often laid with dry joints and the only mortar used was a type of vegetable-based adhesive. Bricks were sometimes carved in situ and occasionally plastered. In the early temples sandstone was only used for architectural embellishments. But nearly all of the later temples were built entirely of sandstone. Most of the sandstone is thought to have been quarried from the northern hills around Kulen and brought by barge to Angkor.

The post-Angkor period was characterized by wooden buildings and fastidiously carved and decorated sculptures, but the humid climate has allowed little to survive. The contemporary art of 21st-century Cambodia is still redolent of the grandeur of the Angkor era and today, Khmer craftsmen retain their inherent skills and are renowned for their refined carvings. Art historians believe that the richness of Cambodia's heritage, and its incorporation into the modern artistic psyche, has enabled Khmer artists to produce work which is reckoned to be aesthetically superior to contemporary carving and sculpture in Thailand.

Textiles

Cambodia is not well known for the quality and range of its textiles, especially when compared with the industry in neighbouring Thailand and Laos. In Chou Ta-kuan's account of life at Angkor written in 1296-1297, he claimed that "Not only do the Khmer women lack skill with needle and thread for mending and sewing, they only know how to weave fabrics of cotton, not of silk". However by the time the French arrived in the second half of the 19th century, weaving in silk and cotton was well-established. The Cambodian royal court had a large retinue of weavers producing sumptuous, richly patterned and coloured silk cloth. Even as recently as the 1940s, weaving was still a craft practised in just about every village, and every woman worth her salt was expected to be able to weave. Then, in the 1950s, cheap imported silk and cotton cloth began to undermine the local product and people began to turn to other occupations. One elderly silk weaver, Liv Sa Em, explained in 1995, "you could earn more selling cakes in two days than you could earn weaving in five months". But it was the Khmer Rouge period which finally sealed the fate of Cambodia's textile industry. Apart from producing the familiar checked cloth used as a head scarf, or *kramar*, weaving virtually died out between 1975 and 1979. Many of the most skilled weavers, especially those associated with the Cambodian court, were either murdered or fled the country. Now the government and many NGOs see a bright future for silk weaving and resources are being directed towards its revitalization. Many women find weaving attractive: it can be built around the demands of housework and childcare; it can be done at home; and it can provide an important supplementary source of income. However, because the domestic industry was so withered after years of neglect, NGOs are finding it necessary to bring in foreign weaving experts from Thailand, Laos, Vietnam and China to teach people anew how to raise silkworms and train women in more advanced weaving techniques.

The Cambodian national dress is the samphot, a long rectangle of cloth (about twice as long as a sarong) which is wrapped around the body and then taken up between the legs to be tucked in at the waist. Traditionally women wore this with a simple breast cloth and men with a jacket. Samphot are woven in rich, warm colours. Sometimes the warp and weft are different colours giving the finished cloth a shimmering appearance. Weft ikat is used to produce the well-known samphot hol and it is thought that this process influenced Thai designs after Siam conquered Angkor in the mid-15th century, taking many of the most skilled weavers back to the capital, Ayutthaya, as booty.

Dance, drama and music

There is a strong tradition of dance in Cambodia which has its origins in the sacred dances of the apsaras, the mythological seductresses of ancient Cambodia. Classical dance reached its height during the Angkor period; it was based on interpretations of the Indian epics, particularly the *Ramayana*. Dance also became a religious tradition, designed to bring the king and his people divine blessing. Dancers, nearly all of whom were well born, were central to the royal court and were protected as a separate part of the king's harem; only the god-king could touch them. The dancers became legendary even outside Cambodia: when Thailand invaded, the Khmer classical ballet dancers were part of their war booty and were taken to the Thai court. The decline of Angkor brought the decline of classical dance, although it continued to survive as an art form through the patronage of the royal Thai court. When the French colonialists revived Khmer ballet in the 20th century they initially imported dancers from Thailand.

The dances are very symbolic. Court dances are subject to a precise order, a strict form and a prescribed language of movements and gestures. Most of the dancers are women and the male and female roles are distinguished by costume. All the dancers are barefoot as the unimpeded movement of the feet is very important. The national dance is called the lamthon which is characterized by slow graceful movements of the hands and arms. The most highly trained lamthon dancers wear elaborate, tight-fitting costumes of silk and velvet that have to be sewn onto them before each performance.

Due to their close association with the royal family (they were based at the royal palace right up to 1970 and danced regularly for Prince Sihanouk), the once-famous and flourishing National Dance Group was a prime target for the Khmer Rouge regime of the mid-1970s. Many dancers were killed; others fled into exile. Em Tiay was one of the few to survive the killing fields. She began dancing at the age of six in 1937 and the only reason she survived the Pol Pot years was because the headman of the village where she lived was so captivated by her dancing that he protected her. Her two sisters were not so lucky. With the fall of the Khmer Rouge she returned to dancing and became a full-time classical dance teacher at the Bassac Theatre in Phnom Penh. In 1981 the School of Fine Arts was reopened to train new recruits, 80% of whom were orphans. Today the National Dance Group, which made its first tour to the West in 1990, performs for some tour groups.

The government, with the help of overseas cultural groups, has been trying to resurrect Cambodia's classical dance tradition. By 1997 about 50% of the classical Khmer dance repertoire had been recovered. Support has come in from sources as diverse as the Japanese city of Fukuoka and UNESCO. Some 80 elderly Khmer who managed to survive the Khmer Rouge holocaust are being interviewed and their knowledge committed to paper while 4000 dance gestures and positions have been recorded on video. Nonetheless the effort is proving difficult.

Folk dancing has managed to survive the 1970s intact, although as a form of regular village entertainment, it has been undermined by the arrival of TV and video. Unlike the court dances, folk dances are less structured, with dancers responding to the rhythm of drums. The dancers act out tales from Cambodian folk stories; folk dancing can often be seen at local festivals.

Folk plays and shadow plays (nang sbaek) are also a popular form of entertainment in the countryside. The latter are based on stories from the *Ramayana*, embroidered with local legends. The characters are cut out of leather and often painted. Wandering shadow puppeteers perform at local festivals.

Because of the importance of dance to the ancient royal Khmer court, music – which always accompanied dance routines – was also central to Cambodian court and religious life. Singers and musicians were often attached to specific temples. Cambodian music has evolved from Indian and Indonesian influences and, more recently, Thai. The traditional orchestra consists of three xylophones, khom thom (a horseshoe-shaped arrangement with 16 flat gongs), violins, wind instruments including flutes, flageolets and a Khmer version of bagpipes, as well as drums of different shapes and sizes. There are three types of drum: the hand drum, the cha ayam drum and the yike drum. The drummer has the most important role in folk music as he sets the rhythm. In 1938 a musical scholar estimated that only 3000 melodies were ever employed in Khmer music. There is no system of written notation so the tunes are transmitted orally from generation to generation. There are five tones (compared to seven in Western music) and no real harmony – the melodies are always simple.

The Cambodian Ramayana: the *Reamker*

The *Reamker* – 'The Story of Rama' – is an adaptation of the Indian Hindu classic, the *Ramayana*, which was written by the poet Valmiki about 2000 years ago. This 48,000 line epic odyssey – often likened to the works of Homer – was introduced into mainland Southeast Asia in the early centuries of the first millennium. The heroes were simply transposed into a mythical, ancient, Southeast Asian landscape.

In Cambodia, the *Reamker* quickly became highly influential. The scenes carved in stone at Angkor, many of the murals painted on monastery walls, and the tales enacted in shadow theatre (*nang sbaek*) all derive inspiration from the *Reamker*. The Cambodian *Ramayana* dates back to the Angkor period, although the earliest existing written work only dates back to 1620.

In the first part of the story, Rama – who in the Cambodian version is depicted as the Buddha – renounces his throne following a long and convoluted court intrigue, and flees into exile. With his wife Sita and trusted companion Hanuman (the monkey god), they undertake a long and arduous journey. In the second part, his wife Sita is abducted by the evil king Ravana, forcing Rama to wage battle against the demons of Langka Island (Sri Lanka). He defeats the demons with the help of Hanuman and his monkey army, and recovers his wife. In the third and final part of the story – and here it diverges sharply from the Indian original – Sita and Rama are reunited and reconciled with the help of the gods (in the Indian version there is no such reconciliation). Another difference from the Indian version is the significant role played by Hanuman – here an amorous adventurer who dominates much of the third part of the epic.

There are also numerous sub-plots which are original to the *Reamker*, many building upon events in Cambodian history and local myth and folklore. In tone and issues of morality, the Cambodian version is less puritanical than the Indian original. There are also, of course, differences in dress, ecology, location and custom.

Adapted from Hallet, Holt (1890) *A thousand miles on an elephant in the Shan States*, William Blackwood: Edinburgh

Hanuman

Religion

The god-kings of Angkor

Until the 14th century Buddhism and Hinduism existed side-by-side in Kambuja. In the pre-Angkor era, the Hindu gods Siva and Vishnu were worshipped as a single deity, Harihara. The statue of Harihara from Phnom Da (eighth century) is divided in half: the 'stern' right half is Siva (with wild curly hair) and the 'sublime' left half, Vishnu (who wears a mitre). The first city at Angkor, built by Jayavarman II in the early ninth century, was called Hariharalaya after this god. Early Angkor kings promoted various Hindu sects, mainly dedicated to Siva and Vishnu. During the Angkor period, Siva was the most favoured deity but by the 12th century Vishnu replaced him. Jayavarman VII introduced Mahayana Buddhism as the official court religion at the end of the 12th century. The constant chopping, changing and refining of state religion helped sustain the power of the absolute monarch – each change ushered in a new style of rule and historians believe refinements and changes of religion were deliberately imported to consolidate the power of the kings.

One reason the Khmer Empire was so powerful was its basis on the Hindu concept of the god-king or devaraja. Jayavarman II (AD 802-850) crowned himself as a reincarnation of Siva and erected a Siva lingam (a phallic monument to the god) at Phnom Kulen, the source of power for the Khmer Dynasty. Siva-worship was not originally introduced by Jayavarman II, however – it had been previously practised in the old kingdom of Funan. The investiture of power was always performed by a Brahmin priest who also bestowed divinity on the king as a gift from Siva. This ceremony became an essential rite of kingship which was observed continuously – right into the 20th century. The king's spirit was said to reside in the lingam, which was enshrined in the centre of a monumental religious complex, representing the spiritual axis of the kingdom. Here, the people believed, their divinely ordained king communicated with the gods. Succeeding monarchs followed Jayavarman II's example and continued to install themselves as god-kings, evoking the loyalty of their subjects.

Very few of the statues of Vishnu and Siva and other gods left by the Khmer Empire were traditional representations of the deities. The great majority of the images were portraits of kings and princes and high dignitaries, each represented as the god into whom they would be absorbed at the end of their earthly existence. That the names given to the statues were usually a composite of the names of the man and the god, indicates that men were worshipped as gods.

The installation of the devaraja cult by Jayavarman II took place on the summit of Phnom Kulen. Under subsequent kings, it was transferred, in turn, to Bakong, Phnom Bakheng, Koh Ker and Phimeanakas. At the end of the 11th century, the Baphuon was constructed to house the golden lingam. The tradition of the god-king cult was so deeply rooted in the court that even Theravada Buddhism introduced in the 14th century bowed to its influence. Following the adoption of Mahayana Buddhism in the second half of the 12th century, the god-king left his lingam to enter the statue of the Buddha. Jayavarman VII built the Bayon to shelter the statue of the Buddha-king in the centre of the city of Angkor.

Temple-mountains were built as microcosms of the universe, with Mount Meru, the home of the gods, at the centre, surrounded by oceans (followed most perfectly at Angkor Wat, see page 14). This concept was not invented by the Khmers but was part of an inherited tradition from India. At the summit of the cosmic mountain, at the centre of the city, the king, embodied by his own sacred image, entered into contact with the world of gods. Each temple was the personal temple of an individual king, erected by him during his life. When, after his death, his ashes or remains were deposited there (to animate the statue and give the cult a living image), the temple became his mausoleum. His successor always built another sanctuary to house the image of the god-king. During the Angkor period the Khmers did not seem to question this system. It ordered their lives, regulating everything from agriculture to birth and death rites. But the temples were not the products of a popular faith, like Christian cathedrals – they were strictly the domain of royalty and high priests and were reserved for the worship of kings and members of the entourage deified in the form of one of the Hindu or Buddhist gods.

Theravada Buddhism

Despite the powerful devaraja cult, most Khmers also practised an amalgam of ancestor worship and animism. As Theravada Buddhism swept through Southeast Asia (well after the adoption of Mahayana Buddhism), propagated by missionary monks, its message of simplicity, austerity and humility began to undermine the cult of the god-king. As a popular religion, it had great attractions for a population which for so many centuries had been denied access to the élitist and extravagant devaraja cult. By the 15th century Theravada Buddhism was the dominant religion in Cambodia.

Buddhism shares the belief, in common with Hinduism, in rebirth. A person goes through countless lives and the experience of one life is conditioned by the acts in a previous one. This is the Law of Karma (act or deed, from Pali kamma), the law of cause and effect. For most people, nirvana is a distant goal, and they merely aim to accumulate merit by living good lives and performing good deeds such as giving alms to monks. In this way the layman embarks on the Path to Heaven. It is also common for a layman to become ordained, at some point in his life (usually as a young man), for a three-month period during the Buddhist Rains Retreat.

Monks should endeavour to lead stringently ascetic lives. They must refrain from murder, theft, sexual intercourse, untruths, eating after noon, alcohol, entertainment, ornament, comfortable beds and wealth. They are allowed to own only a begging bowl, three pieces of clothing, a razor, needle, belt and water filter. They can only eat food that they have received through begging. Anyone who is male, over 20, and not a criminal can become a monk.

The 'Way of the Elders' is believed to be closest to Buddhism as it originally developed in India. It is often referred to by the term 'Hinayana' (Lesser Vehicle), a disparaging name foisted onto Theravadans by Mahayanists. This form of Buddhism is the dominant contemporary religion in the mainland Southeast Asian countries of Thailand, Cambodia, Laos and Burma.

In Theravadan Buddhism, the historic Buddha, Sakyamuni, is revered above all else and most images of the Buddha are of Sakyamuni. Importantly, and unlike Mahayana Buddhism, the Buddha image is only meant to serve as a meditation aid. In theory, it does not embody supernatural powers, and it is not supposed to be worshipped. But the popular need for objects of veneration has meant that most images are worshipped. Pilgrims bring flowers and incense, and prostrate themselves in front of the image. This is a Mahayanist influence which has been embraced by Theravadans.

Buddhism in Cambodia

The Cambodian Buddhist clergy divide into two groups: the Mahanikay and Thommayuth (or Dhammayuttikanikay) orders. The latter was not introduced from Thailand until 1864, and was a reformist order with strong royal patronage. Theravada Buddhism remained the dominant and unchallenged faith until 1975. It was a demonstration by Buddhist monks in Phnom Penh which first kindled Cambodian nationalism in the wake of the Second World War. According to historians, one of the reasons for this was the intensifying of the relationship between the king and the people, due to the founding of the Buddhist Institute in Phnom Penh in 1930. The Institute was under the joint patronage of the kings of Laos and Cambodia as well as the French. It began printing and disseminating Buddhist texts – in Pali and Khmer. Historian David P Chandler wrote: "As the Institute's reputation grew, enhanced by frequent conferences, it became a rallying point for an emerging intelligentsia." The institute's librarian founded a Khmer-language newspaper (Nagaravatta – or 'Angkor Wat') in 1936, which played a critical role in articulating and spreading the nationalist message.

Before 1975 and the arrival of the Khmer Rouge, there were 3000 monasteries and 64,000 monks (bonzes) – many of these were young men who had become ordained to escape conscription – in Cambodia and rural life was centred around the wat (Buddhist monastery). Under Pol Pot, all monks were 'defrocked' and, according to some sources, as many as 62,000 were executed or died in the ricefields. Monasteries were torn down or converted to other uses, Pali – the language of Theravada Buddhism – was banned, and former monks were forced to marry. Ironically, Saloth Sar (Pol Pot) himself spent some time as a novice when he was a child. Buddhism was revived in 1979 with the ordination of monks by a visiting delegation of Buddhists from Vietnam; at the same time, many of the wats – which were defiled by the Khmer Rouge – were restored and reconsecrated. The two orders of Theravada Buddhism – the Thommayuth (aristocratic) and Mahanikay (common) – previously practised in Cambodia have now merged. The Hun Sen government softened the position on Buddhism to the degree that it was reintroduced as the national religion in 1989 and young men were allowed to be ordained (previously restricted to men over 45 that were no longer able to serve in the army).

Today 90% of Cambodian citizens are Buddhist. In 2004, the country had almost 59,500 monks spread across the country's 3980 wats. Cambodian Buddhism is an easy-going faith and tolerates ancestor and territorial spirit worship, which is widely practised. The grounds usually consist of a vihara (Buddhist temple), Sala Thoama saphea (the hall where Dharma is taught) and kods (the quarters where the monks live). Traditionally, the vihara and the Buddha statues contained within them will face east in order to express gratitude to Lord Buddha for enlightenment and guide others toward the path of enlightenment. There are often small rustic altars to the guardian spirits (*neak ta*) in the corner of pagodas. Cambodians often wear *katha* – or charms – which are believed to control external magical forces. Most important ceremonies – weddings, funerals, coming of age – have both Buddhist and animist elements. Wats play an important role in education and it is fairly common to find schools built inside or beside wats.

Other religions

There are around 60,000 Roman Catholics in Cambodia, mainly Vietnamese, and about 2000 Protestants. Islam, of the Sunni sect, is practised by many of the 200,000 (some commentators would say 500,000) Cham. During the Khmer Rouge period it was reported that Cham were forced to eat pork while most Cham mosques were destroyed, and only now are they being slowly rebuilt. An International Mosque in Phnom Penh, built with Saudi money, was opened in 1994. Almost all the Chinese in Cambodia are Taoist/Confucianist.Jacobson, Matt *Adventure Cambodia* (Silkworm Books, 2005, 2nd edition). A good guide for people interested in motorcycling through Cambodia.

Mudras and the Buddha image

An artist producing an image of the Buddha does not try to create an original piece of art; he is trying to be faithful to a tradition which can be traced back over centuries. It is important to appreciate that the Buddha image is not merely a work of art but an object of and for, worship. Sanskrit poetry even sets down the characteristics of the Buddha – albeit in rather unlikely terms: legs like a deer, arms like an elephant's trunk, a chin like a mango stone and hair like the stings of scorpions. The Pali texts of Theravada Buddhism add the 108 auspicious signs, long toes and fingers of equal length, body like a banyan tree and eyelashes like a cow's. The Buddha can be represented either sitting, lying (indicating *paranirvana*), or standing, and (in Thailand) occasionally walking. He is often represented standing on an open lotus flower: the Buddha was born into an impure world, and likewise the lotus germinates in mud but rises above the filth to flower. Each image will be represented in a particular mudra or 'attitude', of which there are 40. The most common are:

Abhayamudra – dispelling fear or giving protection; right hand (sometimes both hands) raised, palm outwards, usually with the Buddha in a standing position.

Varamudra – giving blessing or charity; the right hand pointing downwards, the palm facing outwards, with the Buddha either seated or standing.

Vitarkamudra – preaching mudra; the ends of the thumb and index finger of the right hand touch to form a circle, symbolizing the Wheel of Law. The Buddha can either be seated or standing.

Dharmacakramudra – 'spinning the Wheel of Law'; a preaching mudra symbolizing the teaching of the first sermon. The hands are held in front of the chest, thumbs and index fingers of both joined, one facing inwards and one outwards.

Bhumisparcamudra – 'calling the earth goddess to witness' or 'touching the earth'; the right hand rests on the right knee with the tips of the fingers 'touching ground', thus calling the earth goddess Dharani/Thoranee to witness his enlightenment and victory over Mara, the king of demons. The Buddha is always seated.

Dhyanamudra – meditation; both hands resting open, palms upwards, in the lap, right over left.

Other points of note:

Vajrasana – yogic posture of meditation; cross-legged, both soles of the feet visible.

Virasana – yogic posture of meditation; cross-legged, but with the right leg on top of the left, covering the left foot (also known as *paryankasana*).

Buddha under Naga – the Buddha is shown in an attitude of meditation with a cobra rearing up over his head.

Buddha calling for rain – the Buddha is depicted standing, both arms held stiffly at the side of the body, fingers pointing downwards.

Bhumisparcamudra – calling the earth goddess to witness.
Sukhothai period, 13th-14th century.

Dhyanamudra – meditation.
Sukhothai period, 13th-14th century.

Abhayamudra – dispelling fear or giving protection. Lopburi Buddha, Khmer style 12th century.

Vitarkamudra – preaching, "spinning the Wheel of Law". Dvaravati Buddha, 7th-8th century, seated in the "European" manner.

Abhayamudra – dispelling fear or giving protection; subduing Mara position. Lopburi Buddha, Khmer style 13th century.

The Buddha 'Calling for rain'.

Practicalities
Cambodia

Getting there

Air

International connections with Cambodia are still poor – but improving – and most travellers will need to route themselves through Kuala Lumpur, Singapore or Bangkok, all of which have good onward connections to both Phnom Penh and Siem Reap. There are direct flights only from within the region.

Bangkok is the cheapest gateway to Cambodia from outside the region and offers the best flight connections with Phnom Penh and Siem Reap. **Bangkok Airways** offers a regional 'Discovery Airpass' which includes **Siem Reap Airways** routes.

To/from Phnom Penh These airlines currently operate international services to Phnom Penh's Pochentong Airport: **Air Asia** (Kuala Lumpur, Bangkok); **Bangkok Airways** (Bangkok); **China Airlines** (Taipei); **Silk Air** (Singapore); **Dragon Air** (Hong Kong); **Thai** (Bangkok); **Malaysia Airlines** (Kuala Lumpur); **Vietnam Airlines** (Vientiane, Ho Chi Minh City); **Shanghai Air** (Shanghai); **China Southern** (Guangzhou); **Eva** (Taipei); **Jet Star** (Singapore); **Korean & Asiana** (Incheon). The Cambodian national flag carrier **Cambodia Angkor Air** flies to and from Ho Chi Minh City.

To/from Siem Reap There are connections with **Bangkok Airways** (Bangkok); **Air Asia** (Kuala Lumpur); **Malaysia** (Kuala Lumpur); **Vietnam** (Hanoi and Ho Chi Minh City); **Jet Star** (Singapore); **Silk** (Singapore); **Korean & Asiana** (Incheon); **Lao Aviation** (Vientiane).

Rail

There are currently no passenger rail services running in Cambodia, though plans are emerging for routes to reopen.

River

There are sailings from Ho Chi Minh City (Vietnam) to Phnom Penh. Ho Chi Minh City tour operators run minibuses to Chau Doc and on to the border, which is crossed on foot. Change to a speed boat which will take you to Neak Luong in Cambodia. Disembark here and take a taxi/pickup along Route 1 to Phnom Penh.

Road

You can enter Cambodia, overland, from Thailand, Vietnam and Laos. Travellers coming from Thailand usually cross at **Poipet** where they'll find a recently completed fast road to Siem Reap. There are now overland entries from Thailand through **Pailin** (very rough roads) and **Koh Kong**, where new roads have also been completed (the boat from Koh Kong to Sihanoukville no longer operates). The overland route from Vietnam via **Moc Bai** is the slow but cheap option for travellers coming from the east, and the border crossing at **Omsano** has enabled those coming from Vietnam to take the more scenic river route via Chau Doc. There is a new scenic border open via Kep between Cambodia and Vietnam (**Ha Tien**). There is also a crossing between Phnom Penh and **Tinh Bien** in Vietnam.

Getting around

Air

If time is limited, by far the best option is to get an open-jaw flight where you fly into one city and out of another or fly into Bangkok, the cheapest point of entry, and use the **Bangkok Airways** regional 'Discovery Airpass', which includes **Siem Reap Airways** routes. Distances between towns are long and roads are not always sealed, making overland journey times lengthy and sometimes tortuous, especially in the wet season.

At the moment the only domestic route within Cambodia that operates safely and with any frequency is between Phnom Penh and Siem Reap. National carrier, **Cambodia Angkor Air**, flies this route but its website, www.cambodiaangkorair. com, doesn't allow bookings; their office in Phnom Penh is at 1-2/294 Mao Tse Tung, T023-666 6786. All departure taxes are now included in your fare.

Road

Over the last few years the road system in Cambodia has dramatically improved. A trunk route of international standards, apart from a few bumpy stretches, from Stung Treng to Koh Kong is due for completion in the near future. Much of the rest of the network is pretty basic and journeys can sometimes be long and laborious. Also, to some parts, such as Ratanakiri, the road is a graded laterite track, unpaved and potholed. In the rainy season expect to be slowed down on many roads to a slithering muddy crawl. The Khmer-American Friendship Highway (Route 4), which runs from Phnom Penh to Sihanoukville, is entirely paved, as is the National Highway 6 between Siem Reap and Phnom Penh. The infamous National Highway 6 between Poipet and Phnom Penh via Siem Reap has also had extensive work, as has National Highway 1. The Japanese in particular have put considerable resources into road and bridge building.

Bus and shared taxi There are buses and shared taxis to most parts of the country. Shared taxis are not as common as they used to be. The taxi operators charge a premium for better seats and you can buy yourself more space. It is not uncommon for a taxi to fit 10 people in it, including two sitting on the driver's seat. Fares for riding in the back of the truck are half that for riding in the cab. The Sihanoukville run has an excellent and cheap air-conditioned bus service.

Car hire and taxi A few travel agents and hotels may be able to organize self-drive car hire and most hotels have cars for hire with a driver (US$30-50 per day). There is a limited taxi service in Phnom Penh.

Moto and tuk-tuk The most popular and sensible options are the motorbike taxi, known as 'moto', and the tuk-tuk. They costs around the same as renting your own machine and with luck you will get a driver who speaks a bit of English and who knows where he's going. Once you have found a good driver stick with him. Outside Phnom Penh and Siem Reap, do not expect much English from your moto/tuk-tuk driver.

Motorbike and bicycle hire Motorbikes can be rented from between US$5 and US$8 per day and around US$1 for a bicycle. If riding either a motorbike or a bicycle be aware that the accident fatality rate is very high. This is partly because of the poor condition of many of the vehicles on the road; partly because of the poor roads; and partly because of the horrendously poor driving. If you do rent a motorbike ensure it has a working horn (imperative) and buy some rear-view mirrors so you can keep an eye on the traffic. Wear a helmet (even if using a motodop).

River

All the Mekong towns and settlements around the Tonlé Sap are accessible by boat. It is a very quick and relatively comfortable way to travel and much cheaper than flying. The route between Siem Reap and Phnom Penh is very popular, while the route between Siem Reap and Battambang is one of the most scenic. With the new road opening, boats are no longer used as a main form of transport along the Mekong and in the northeast.

Maps

Country maps *Gecko Maps* (1:750,000), highly recommended. *Periplus Cambodia* (1: 1,100,000); *Nelles Vietnam, Laos and Cambodia* (1:1,500,000); *Bartholomew Vietnam, Laos and Cambodia* (1:2,000,000).

City maps The *Periplus Cambodia* map also has a good map of Phnom Penh (1:17,000) and a detailed map of Angkor (1:95,000). *Gecko Maps* (1:750,000) has a good map of Siem Reap, Sihanoukville and Phnom Penh. There is a 3D map of Siem Reap and Phnom Penh, which is quite good and is distributed for free in restaurants, bars and guesthouses.

Other maps *Tactical Pilotage Charts* (TPC, US Airforce) (1:500,000); *Operational Navigational Charts* (ONC, US Airforce) (1:500,000). Both of these are particularly good at showing relief features (useful for planning treks); less good on roads, towns and facilities.

Where to stay
in Cambodia

Accommodation standards in Cambodia have greatly improved over the last couple of years. Phnom Penh now has a good network of genuine boutique hotels – arguably they are overpriced and sometimes management can be a bit Fawlty Towers but the bar has certainly been raised. Siem Reap, without doubt, has now become a destination for the upmarket international traveller. The range, depth and quality of accommodation here is of an excellent standard and is on a par with anywhere else in Asia. Even if you travel to some of the smaller, less-visited towns, family-run Chinese-style hotels should now provide hot water, air conditioning and cable TV even if they can't provide first-class service. These places are often the best bargains in the country as many of the cheap backpacker places, while very, very cheap, are mostly hovels.

More expensive hotels have safety boxes in the rooms. In cheaper hotels it is not uncommon for things to be stolen from bedrooms. In Phnom Penh this poses a real dilemma for it is more dangerous to take valuables on to the night time streets. Most hotels and guesthouses will accept valuables for safekeeping but do keep a close eye on your cash.

Price codes

Where to stay	Restaurants
$$$$ over US$100	$$$ over US$12
$$$ US$46-100	$$ US$6-12
$$ US$21-45	$ under US$6
$ US$20 and under	Prices refer to the cost of a two-course meal not including drinks.
Prices refer to the cost of a standard double/twin room in high season.	

Food & drink
in Cambodia

For a country that has suffered and starved in the way Cambodia has, eating for fun as opposed to for survival, has yet to catch on as a pastime. There are some good restaurants and things are improving but don't expect Cambodia to be a smaller version of Thailand, or its cuisine even to live up to the standards of Laos. Cambodian food shows clear links with the cuisines of neighbouring countries: Thailand, Vietnam and, to a lesser extent, Laos. The influence of the French colonial period is also in evidence, most clearly in the availability of good French bread. Chinese food is also available owing to strong business ties between Cambodia and China. True Khmer food is difficult to find and much that the Khmers would like to claim as indigenous food is actually of Thai, French or Vietnamese origin. Curries, soups, rice and noodle-based dishes, salads, fried vegetables and sliced meats all feature in Khmer cooking.

Drink
International **soft drinks** are widely available in Cambodia. If there is a national drink in Cambodia, then it has to be **tea,** which is drunk without sugar or milk. **Coffee** is also available black or 'crème' with sweetened condensed milk. Soda water with lemon, *soda kroch chhmar*, is a popular drink. **Bottled water** is widely available; local mineral water too. Most market stands will serve great **fruit smoothies**, but you might wish to request less sugar and minimal sweet milk and stipulate whether you want egg or not. Fresh **milk** is hard to find outside of metropolitan areas. International soft drinks are readily available.

FOOD
Fishy business

Every national cuisine has its signature dish and in Cambodia it is prahok, a strong, pungent, fermented fish paste that's been used to flavour Khmer dishes for centuries. Cambodians swear by it and use it in everything from dips and soups, through to a simple accompaniment for rice. Reports suggest that 95% of Cambodians eat the delicacy, so it is no surprise that the practice of making it has passed down from generation to generation.

The Fisheries Department believe that in some areas 10% of fish caught are set aside for the manufacture of prahok. The paste is made by stomping on hundreds of small fish and fish heads in a large bucket. Once the fish is transformed into a thick brown paste it's left in the sun for a day to ferment. Salt is then added and the paste is put in jars and sold.

Locals suggest that prahok can be eaten after a month of maturation, but most consider the paste to be at its best after a few years. This is a Cambodian delicacy, like sushi or Parmesan cheese, and may taste a bit unusual at first, it is something of an acquired taste (if you can get past the smell).

Local and imported **beers** are also available. Of the locally brewed beers the three most common are Angkor Beer, Anchor and ABC Stout – on draught, in bottles and cans. VB or Victoria Bitter is also brewed locally but is much less common. Beer Lao, although imported, is usually the cheapest and also one of the best.

Eating out

Phnom Penh and Siem Reap have the best restaurants with French, Japanese, Italian and Indian food being available. But those who want to sample a range of dishes and get a feel for Khmer cuisine should head for the nearest market where dishes will be cooked on order in a wok – known locally as a *chhnang khteak*.

Local customs and conduct

Temples When visiting a temple do dress respectfully (keep bare flesh to a minimum) and take off your hat and shoes. When sitting, put your legs to one side and try not to point the soles of your feet at anyone or at the Buddha image. Females are not to touch monks or sit beside them on public transport. A small donation is often appropriate.

Greeting Cambodians use their traditional greeting – the 'wai' – bowing with their hands held together. As a foreigner, shaking hands is perfectly acceptable.

In private homes It is polite to take your shoes off on entering the house and a small present goes down well if you are invited for a meal.

Photography In general, the best time to photograph most temples is before 0900 and after 1630. Don't forget to ask the permission of any people who you wish to include in your shots.

General Displays of anger or exasperation are considered unacceptable and therefore reflect very badly on the individual. Accordingly, even in adversity, Khmers (like the Thais) will keep smiling. Displays of affection should be avoided in public areas. Avoid touching people on the head. To beckon someone, use your hand with the palm facing downwards. Pointing is rude.

Women should dress modestly. Short skirts, and tight or revealing outfits are deemed deemed inappropriate. If you choose to dress like this then you may attract undesirable attention and potentially offend some people.

Essentials A-Z

Accident and emergency

Contact the relevant emergency service and your embassy: **Ambulance** T119/724891, **Fire** T118, **Police** T117/112/012-999999. Obtain police/medical records in order to file insurance claims.

Children

Travelling with children can be a most rewarding experience in Cambodia, and with sufficient care and planning, it can also be safe. Children are often excellent passports into a local culture – the Khmers love babies and children – and you will also receive the best service and help from officials and members of the public if you have kids with you. Be wary of squalid cooking conditions at hotels and market stalls and try to ensure that children do not drink any untreated water (especially important when bathing). Bottled water and fizzy drinks are widely available.

For babies, powdered milk is available in provincial centres, although most brands have added sugar. Baby food can also be bought in some towns – the quality may not be the same as equivalent foods bought in the West, but it is perfectly adequate for short periods. Disposable nappies can be bought in Phnom Penh, but are often expensive.

Customs and duty free

Roughly 200 cigarettes or the equivalent quantity of tobacco, 1 bottle of liquor and perfume for personal use can be taken out of the country without incurring customs duty. Taking any Angkorian-era images out of the country is strictly forbidden.

Disabled travellers

Cambodia may have the world's highest incidence of one-legged and no-legged people (because of landmine injuries) but this does not mean that facilities for the disabled are well developed. In short, Cambodia is not an easy country for the disabled traveller: pavements are often uneven, there are potholes galore, pedestrian crossings are ignored, ramps are unheard of and lifts are few and far between. On top of this, numerous other hazards abound, among the most dangerous of which must number the taxi and moto drivers whose philosophy on road safety is eccentric to say the least. However, while there are scores of hurdles that disabled people will have to negotiate, the Cambodians themselves are likely to go out of their way to be helpful.

Drugs

As Amit Gilboa's book, *Off the Rails in Phnom Penh*, makes clear, drugs are readily available and cheap in Cambodia. Many places use marijuana in their cooking and the police seem to be quite ambivalent to dope smokers (unless they need to supplement their income with your bribe money, in which case – watch out). Drugs (including marijuana) are illegal, so there is always a legal risk if you wish to indulge.

Without exaggeration, one of the

biggest dangers for travellers who take drugs in Cambodia today is dying of an overdose. You run a much higher risk of this than of being shot, beaten, blown up by a landmine or other 'dangers' associated with this 'Off the Rails' lifestyle. Travellers are the highest risk group when it comes to drug overdoses (or at least the group most reported). The backpacker areas around the lake in Phnom Penh and Sihanoukville are particularly prone to the problem, with travellers being pulled dead from seedy guesthouses week in week out.

The frequency of overdoses is largely attributed to the fact that the people buying drugs aren't getting what they thought they were. It is believed that most people found dead (by overdose) thought they had bought ecstasy or cocaine but had in fact been given heroin. It is important to note that cocaine and ecstasy do not really exist in Cambodia, despite what you may be told.

Another particularly nasty side effect from the drugs explosion in Cambodia is the introduction of yaa baa. Although the drug has been around the region for a while it really has taken a stranglehold on Cambodia, especially in urban areas. It is a particularly nasty amphetamine that is said to have sent numerous people mad and can also be lethal.

In a nutshell: don't buy illicit drugs in Cambodia, it is dangerous.

Electricity

Voltage 220. Sockets are usually round 2-pin.

Embassies and consulates

A full list of Cambodian embassies and consulates can be found at http://embassygoabroad.com.

Festivals and public holidays

January

1 and 7 Jan New Year's Day (public holiday), National Day and Victory over Pol Pot (public holiday). Celebration of the fall of the Khmer Rouge in 1979. It is also the anniversary of the beginning of the Vietnamese occupation of the country, leading some people to lobby against it being declared a national holiday.

Jan/Feb Chinese and Vietnamese New Year (movable). Celebrated by the Chinese and Vietnamese communities. Anniversary of the last sermon of Buddha (movable).

March

8 Mar International Women's Day (public holiday). Processions, floats and banners in main towns.

April

13-15 Apr Cambodian New Year or Bonn Chaul Chhnam (public holiday). A 3-day celebration to mark the turn of the year. Predictions are made for the forthcoming year, the celebration is to show gratitude to the departing demi-god and to welcome the new one. Every household erects a small altar filled with offerings of food and drink to welcome a new demi-god. Homes are spring cleaned. Householders visit temples and traditional games like *boh angkunh* and *chhoal chhoung* are played and rituals are performed.

17 Apr Independence Day (public holiday). Celebrates the fall of the Lon Nol government (17 Apr 1975) with floats and parades through Phnom Penh.
Chaul Chhnam (movable). 3-day celebration, which involves an inevitable drenching, to welcome in the new year. It's a similar festival to Pimai in Laos and Songkran in Thailand.

April/May
Visak Bauchea (movable – full moon, public holiday). The most important Buddhist festival; a triple anniversary commemorating Buddha's birth, enlightenment and his Paranirvana (state of final bliss).

May
1 May Labour Day.
9 May Genocide Day (public holiday). To remember the atrocities of the Khmer Rouge rule, during which nearly 2 million Cambodians lost their lives. The main ceremony is held at Choeng Ek, just south of Phnom Penh.
Royal Ploughing Ceremony (movable, public holiday). As in Thailand, this marks the beginning of the rainy season and traditionally is meant to alert farmers to the fact that the job of rice cultivation is set to begin (as if farmers need any advance warning!). Known as *bonn chroat preah nongkoal* in Khmer, the ceremony is held on a field close to the Royal Palace in Phnom Penh. The land is ploughed by a man (King of Meakh) while the seed is sown by a woman (Queen Me Hour), reflecting the gender division of labour in agriculture and probably also symbolizing fertility. The sacred cows are led to silver trays holding rice, corn and other foods. Their choice of food is taken as an omen for the coming year.

June
1 Jun International Children's Day.
18 Jun Her Majesty Preah Akkaek Mohesey Norodom Monineath Sihanouk's Birthday.
19 Jun Anniversary of the Founding of the Revolutionary Armed Forces of Kampuchea (1951). The main parades and celebrations are in Phnom Penh.
28 Jun Anniversary of the founding of the People's Revolutionary Party of Cambodia (1951). The main parades and celebrations are in Phnom Penh.

July
Chol Vassa (moveable with the full moon). The start of the rainy season retreat – a Buddhist 'lent' – for meditation. It is the most important Buddhist festival; a triple anniversary commemorating Buddha's birth, enlightenment and his Paranirvana (state of final bliss).

September
End of Buddhist 'lent' (movable). In certain areas it is celebrated with boat races.
Prachum Ben (movable, public holiday), Ancestors' Day, in remembrance of the dead. Offerings are made to the ancestors.
24 Sep Constitution Day.

October/November
Oct/Nov Water Festival, Bon Om Tuk (movable, public holiday) or **Festival of the Reversing Current**. To celebrate the movement of the waters out of the Tonlé Sap (see page 44), boat races are held in Phnom Penh. The festival dates back to the 12th century when King Jayavarman VII and his navy defeated water-borne invaders. Most wats have ceremonial canoes which are rowed by

the monks to summon the Naga King. Boat races extend over 3 days with more than 200 competitors but the highlight is the evening gala in Phnom Penh when a fleet of boats, studded with lights, row out under the full moon. Under the Cambodian monarchy, the king would command the waters to retreat. The festival was only revived in 1990. In addition to celebrating the reversing of the flow of the Tonlé Sap River, this festival marks the onset of the fishing season. (The Khmer diaspora in Vietnam celebrate the same festival at the same time further down the Mekong in Soc Trang.) The festival coincides with **Ok Ambok** (The Pounding of Rice).

23 Oct **Paris Peace Accord**.

30 Oct-1 Nov **King Sihanouk's Birthday** (public holiday). Public offices and museums close for about a week and a firework display is mounted by the river close to the Royal Palace in Phnom Penh.

November
9 Nov **Independence Day** (public holiday). Marks Cambodia's independence from French colonial rule in 1953.

December
10 Dec **Human Rights Day**.
Late Dec **Half marathon** held at Angkor Wat.

Gay and lesbian

Gay and lesbian travellers will have no problems in Cambodia. Men often hold other men's hands as do women, so this kind of affection is commonplace. Any kind of passionate kissing or sexually orientated affection in public, however, is taboo – both for straight and gay people. The gay scene is just starting to develop in Cambodia but there is definitely a scene in the making. **Linga Bar** in Siem Reap and the **Salt Lounge** in Phnom Penh are both gay bars and are excellent choices for a night out.

Health

See your GP or travel clinic at least 6 weeks before departure for general advice on travel risks and vaccinations. Try phoning a specialist travel clinic if your own doctor is unfamiliar with health conditions in Cambodia. Make sure you have sufficient medical travel insurance, get a dental check, know your own blood group and if you suffer a long-term condition such as diabetes or epilepsy, obtain a **Medic Alert** bracelet/ necklace (www. medicalert.co.uk). If you wear glasses, take a copy of your prescription.

Vaccinations
It is advisable to vaccinate against polio, tetanus, typhoid, hepatitis A, and rabies if going to more remote areas. Yellow fever does not exist in Cambodia, but the authorities may wish to see a certificate if you have recently arrived from an endemic area in Africa or South America. Japanese encephalitis may be advised for some areas, depending on the duration of the trip and proximity to rice-growing and pig-farming areas.

Health risks
The most common cause of travellers' **diarrhoea** is from eating contaminated food. Swimming in sea or river water that has been contaminated by sewage can also be a cause; ask locally if it is safe. Diarrhoea may be also caused by viruses, bacteria (such as E-coli),

protozoal (such as giardia), salmonella and cholera. It may be accompanied by vomiting or by severe abdominal pain. Any kind of diarrhoea responds well to the replacement of water and salts. Sachets of rehydration salts can be bought in most chemists and can be dissolved in boiled water. If the symptoms persist, consult a doctor. Tap water in the major cities is in theory safe to drink but it may be advisable to err on the side of caution and drink only bottled or boiled water. Avoid having ice in drinks unless you trust that it is from a reliable source.

Mosquitoes are more of a nuisance than a serious hazard but some, of course, are carriers of serious diseases such as **malaria**, which exists in most of Cambodia except Phnom Penh. The choice of malaria prophylaxis will need to be something other than chloroquine for most people, since there is such a high level of resistance to it. Always check with your doctor or travel clinic for the most up-to-date advice on the best anti-malarials to use. It's also sensible to avoid being bitten as much as possible. Sleep off the ground and use a mosquito net and some kind of insecticide. Mosquito coils release insecticide as they burn and are available in many shops, as are tablets of insecticide, which are placed on a heated mat plugged into a wall socket.

Each year there is the possibility that **avian flu** or **SARS** might rear their ugly heads. Check the news reports. If there is a problem in an area you are due to visit you may be advised to have an ordinary flu shot or to seek expert advice.

There are high rates of **HIV** in the region, especially among sex workers.

If you get sick

Contact your embassy or consulate for a list of doctors and dentists who speak your language, or at least some English. Make sure you have adequate insurance (see below). Ask at your hotel for a good local doctor. Hospitals are not recommended anywhere in Cambodia (even at some of the clinics that profess to be 'international'). If you fall ill or are injured your best bet is to get yourself quickly to either **Bumrungrad Hospital** or **Bangkok Nursing Home**, both in Bangkok. Both hospitals are of an exceptional standard, even in international terms.

Thailand

Bangkok Nursing Home, 9/1 Convent Rd, Silom Bangkok. T+662 686-2700, www.bnhhospital. com. **Bumrungrad Hospital**, Soi 3 Sukhumvit, Bangkok, T+66 2-667 1000, www.bumrungrad.com.

Useful websites

www.btha.org British Travel Health Association.
www.cdc.gov US government site that gives excellent advice on travel health and details of disease outbreaks.
www.fco.gov.uk British Foreign and Commonwealth Office travel site has useful information on each country, people, climate and a list of UK embassies/consulates.
www.fitfortravel.scot.nhs.uk A-Z of vaccine/health advice for each country.
www.numberonehealth.co.uk Travel screening services, vaccine and travel health advice, email/SMS text vaccine reminders and screens returned travellers for tropical diseases.

Insurance

Always take out travel insurance before you set off and read the small print carefully. Check that the policy covers the activities you intend, or may end up, doing. Also check exactly what your medical cover includes, ie ambulance, helicopter rescue or emergency flights back home. Also check the payment protocol. You may have to cough up first before the insurance company reimburses you. It is always best to dig out all the receipts for expensive personal effects like jewellery or cameras. Take photos of these items and note down all serial numbers. You are advised to shop around. STA Travel, T0871-230 0040, www.statravel.co.uk, and other reputable student travel organizations offer good value policies. Young travellers from North America can try the International Student Insurance Service (ISIS), available through STA Travel, T1-800-7770112, www.sta-travel.com. Older travellers should note that some companies will not cover people over 65 years old, or may charge higher premiums. Please also note your nation's ongoing travel warnings – if you travel to areas or places that are not recommended for travel your insurance may be invalid.

Internet

Wi-Fi is available pretty much everywhere in Cambodia, including cafés and restaurants, and internet shops have now almost closed down.

Language

In Cambodia the national language is Khmer (pronounced 'Khmei'). It is not tonal and the script is derived from the southern Indian alphabet. French is spoken by the older generation who survived the Khmer Rouge era. English is the language of the younger generations. Away from Phnom Penh, Siem Reap and Sihanoukville it can be difficult to communicate with the local population unless you speak Khmer.

Media

Cambodia has a vigorous English-language press that fights bravely for editorial independence and freedom to criticize politicians. The principal English-language newspapers are the fortnightly *Phnom Penh Post*, which many regard as the best, and the *Cambodia Daily*, published 5 times a week. There are also tourist magazine guides.

Money

US$1 = 4060, UK£1 = 6167, €1 = 4681 (Feb 2015)
The riel is the official currency though US dollars are widely accepted and easily exchanged. In Phnom Penh and other towns most goods and services are priced in dollars and there is little need to buy riel. In remote rural areas prices are quoted in riel (except accommodation). Money can be exchanged in banks and hotels. US$ traveller's cheques are easiest to exchange – commission ranges from 1% to 3%. Cash advances on credit cards are available. Credit card facilities are limited but some banks, hotels and restaurants do accept them, mostly in the tourist centres. **ANZ Royal Bank** has opened a number of ATMs throughout Phnom Penh, as well as several in provincial Cambodia. Most machines give US$ only.

Cost of travelling

The budget traveller will find that a little goes a long way. Numerous guesthouses offer accommodation at around US$3-7 a night. Food-wise, the seriously strapped can easily manage to survive healthily on US$4-5 per day, so an overall daily budget (not allowing for excursions) of US$7-9 should be enough or the really cost-conscious. For the less frugally minded, a daily allowance of US$30 should see you relatively well-housed and fed, while at the upper end of the scale, there are, in Phnom Penh and Siem Reap, plenty of restaurants and hotels for those looking for Cambodian levels of luxury. A mid-range hotel (attached bathroom, hot water and a/c) will normally cost around US$25 per night and a good meal at a restaurant around US$5-10.

Opening hours

Bars By law, these close at 2400.
Banks Mon-Fri 0800-1600. Some close 1100-1300. Some major branches are open until 1100 on Sat.
Offices Mon-Fri 0730-1130, 1330-1630.
Restaurants, cafés and bars Daily from 0700-0800 although some open earlier.
Shops Daily from 0800-2000. Some, however, stay open for a further 1-2 hrs, especially in tourist centres. Most markets open daily between 0530/0600-1700.

Police and the law

A vast array of offences are punishable in Cambodia, from minor traffic violations through to possession of drugs (see above). If you are arrested or are having difficulty with the police contact your embassy immediately.

Corruption is a problem and contact with the police should be avoided, unless absolutely necessary. Most services, including the provision of police reports, will require the payment of bribes. Law enforcement is very haphazard, at times completely subjective and justice can be hard to find. Some smaller crimes receive large penalties while perpetrators of greater crimes often get off scot-free.

Post

International service is unpredictable but it is reasonably priced and fairly reliable (at least from Phnom Penh). Only send mail from the GPO in any given town rather than sub POs or mail boxes. **Fedex** and **DHL** also offer services.

Safety

Cambodia is not as dangerous as some would have us believe. The country has really moved forward in protecting tourists and violent crime towards visitors is comparatively low. As Phnom Penh has a limited taxi service, travel after dark poses a problem. Stick to moto drivers you know. Women are particularly targeted by bag snatchers. Khmer New Year is known locally as the 'robbery season'. Theft is endemic at this time of year so be on red alert. A common trick around New Year is for robbers to throw water and talcum powder in the eyes of their victim and rob them. Leave your valuables in the hotel safe or hidden in your room.

Outside Phnom Penh safety is not as much of a problem. Visitors should be very cautious when walking in the countryside, however, as landmines and other unexploded ordnance is a ubiquitous hazard. Stick to well-worn paths, especially around Siem Reap and when visiting remote temples. There is currently unrest on the border with Thailand around the Preah Vihear temple; check the situation before travelling.

Students

There are no specific student discounts in Cambodia. Anyone in full-time education is entitled to an **International Student Identity Card** www.isic.org. These are issued by student travel offices and travel agencies and offer special rates on all forms of transport and other concessions and services. They sometimes permit free admission to museums and sights, at other times a discount on the admission.

Tax

Airport tax In Cambodia the international departure tax is US$25, domestic tax is US$6. Airport departure taxes are now included in air fares.

Telephone

The country code for Cambodia is +855.
Landline linkages are so poor in Cambodia that many people and businesses prefer to use mobile phones instead. If you have an unlocked phone and intend to be in the country for a while, it is relatively easy to buy a sim card. This can save you money if you wish to use your phone regularly. International and domestic Cambodian call charges are relatively cheap. There is an excellent mobile network throughout Cambodia. Most mobile phone numbers begin with 01 or 09. The 3-digit prefix included in a 9-digit

landline telephone number is the area (province) code. If dialling within a province, dial only the 6-digit number.

International calls can be made from most guesthouses, hotels and phone booths but don't anticipate being able to make them outside Phnom Penh, Siem Reap and Sihanoukville. Use public MPTC or Camintel card phone boxes dotted around Phnom Penh to make international calls (cards are usually sold at shops near the booth). International calls are expensive, starting at US$4 per min in Phnom Penh, and more in the provinces. To make an overseas call from Cambodia, dial 007 or 001 + IDD country code + area code minus first 0 + subscriber number. Internet calls are without a doubt the cheapest way to call overseas.

Time

7 hrs ahead of GMT.

Tipping

Tipping is rare but appreciated. Salaries in restaurants and hotels are low and many staff hope to make up the difference in tips. As with everywhere else, good service should be rewarded.

Tourist information

Government tourism services are minimal at best. The **Ministry of Tourism**, 3 Monivong Blvd, T023-426876, is not able to provide any useful information or services. The tourism office in Siem Reap is marginally better but will only provide services, such as guides, maps, etc, for a nominal fee. You are better off going through a private operator for information and price.

Useful websites

www.cambodia.org The Cambodian Information Centre. Wealth of information.

www.embassyofcambodia. org Remarkably good website set up by the Royal Cambodian Embassy in Washington DC. Informative and reasonably up to date.

www.gocambodia.com Useful range of practical information.

www.khmer440.com The forum is very good for bouncing any specific Cambodia questions to the predominantly expat crowd.

www.tourismcambodia. com Cambodia's National Tourism Authority. Good source of general and practical information on travel, visas, accommodation and so on.

www.travel.state.gov Useful information for travellers.

Tour operators

Numerous operators offer organized trips, ranging from a whistle-stop tour of the highlights to specialist trips that focus on a specific activity. The advantage of travelling with a reputable operator is that your transport, accommodation and activities are all arranged for you in advance – particularly valuable if you only have limited time. By travelling independently, however, you can be much more flexible about where you go and what you do. You can explore less visited areas and save money, if you budget carefully. For regional tour operators, such as **Asian Trails**, www.asiantrails.com, refer to the tour operator listings in the guide.

In the UK

Adventure Company, 15 Turk St, Alton, Hampshire GU34 1AG, T0870-794 1009, www.adventurecompany.co.uk.

Audley Travel, 6 Willows Gate, Stratton, Audley, Oxfordshire OX27 9AU, T01869-276219, www.audleytravel.com.

Intrepid Travel, 1 Cross and Pillory Lane, Alton GU34 1HL, T01420 595020, www.intrepidtravel.com.

Magic of the Orient, 14 Frederick Pl, Clifton, Bristol BS8 1AS, T0117-311 6050, www.magicoftheorient.com. Tailor-made holidays to the Far East.

Regent Holidays, 15 John St, Bristol BS1 2HR, T0117-921 1711, www.regent-holidays.co.uk.

See Asia Differently, T020-8150 5150, SeeAsiaDifferently.com. A UK/Asian-based tour company specializing in customized Southeast Asian tours including Cambodia.

Silk Steps, Deep Meadow, Edington, Bridgwater, Somerset TA7 9JH, T01278-722460, www.silksteps.co.uk.

Steppes Travel, 51 Castle St, Cirencester, Glos GL7 1QD, T01285-880980, www.steppestravel.co.uk. Specialists in tailor-made holidays and small group tours.

Symbiosis Expedition Planning, 3B Wilmot Place, London NW1 9JS, T0845-123 2844, www.symbiosis-travel.com.

Trans Indus, Northumberland House, 11 The Pavement, Popes Lane, London W5 4NG, T020-8566 2729, www.transindus.co.uk.

Travelmood, 214 Edgware Rd, London W2 1DH, T0870-001002, www.travelmood.com.

Visit Vietnam (Tennyson Travel), 30-32 Fulham High St, London SW6 3LQ, T020-7736 4347, www.visitvietnam.co.uk. Also deals with Cambodia, www.visitasia.co.uk.

In North America

Adventure Center, 1311 63rd St, Suite 200, Emeryville, CA, T1-800 227 8747, www.adventurecenter.com.

Global Spectrum, 3907 Laro Court, Fairfax, VA 22031, T1-800 419 4446, www.globalspectrumtravel.com.

Hidden Treasure Tours, 162 West Park Av, 2nd Floor, Long Beach, NY 11561, T1-888 889 9906, www.hiddentreasuretours.com.

Journeys, 107 April Drive, Suite 3, Ann Arbor MI 46103, T734-665 4407, www.journeys-intl.com.

Myths & Mountains, 976 Tree Court, Incline Village, NV 89451, T800-670-6984 www.mythsandmountains.com. Organizes travel to Cambodia.

Nine Dragons Travel & Tours, PO Box 24105, Indianapolis, IN 46224, T1-317-329 0350, T1-800 909 9050 (USA toll free), www.nine-dragons.com.

In Australia and New Zealand

Intrepid Travel, 360 Bourke St, Melbourne, Victoria 3000, T03-8602 0500, www.intrepidtravel.com.

Travel Indochina, Level 10, HCS House, 403 George St, Sydney, NSW 2000, T02-9244 2133, T1300-367666 (toll free), www.travelindochina.com.au. Small-group journeys and tailor-made holidays.

In Southeast Asia

Asia Pacific Travel, 127 Ban Co St, District Q3, T+84 (0)91322 4473, www.asiapacifictravel.vn. Arranges tours throughout Vietnam, Cambodia and Laos.

Discovery Indochina, 63A Cua Bac St, Hanoi, Vietnam, T+84 (0)43 716 4132, www.discoveryindochina.com. Private and customized tours covering Cambodia, Vietnam and Laos.

Luxury Travel, 5 Nguyen Truong To St, Ba Dinh District, Hanoi, T+84 (0)4 3927 4120, www.luxurytravelvietnam.com. Luxury tours to Vietnam, Cambodia and Laos, as well as Myanmar and Thailand. Tailor-made itineraries, including golf, family holidays, beach holidays and honeymoons.

Visas and immigration

E-visas

It is now possible to get an e-visa for entry to Cambodia which can be bought, online, before arrival. At present, it is only usable at certain entry and exit points but is likely to be rolled out everywhere in the future. The best thing about this visa is being able to avoid any visa scams etc when arriving at Cambodia's notorious land crossings – at least at those where it can be used.

To apply for an e-visa visit www.evisa.gov.kh. The fee is US$30 plus a US$7 handling fee; it takes 3 working days to process and is valid for 3 months but only for 30 days in Cambodia. There is a list on the website of the entry and exit points where the visa is valid. It can also be extended for 30 days at National Police Immigration Department, Ministry of Interior, 332 Russian Blvd, opposite Phnom Penh International Airport, Phnom Penh, Cambodia. T012-581558, www.immigration.gov.khwww.immigration.gov.kh.

Visas on arrival

Visas for a 30-day stay are available on arrival at Phnom Penh and Siem Reap airport. Tourist visas cost US$30 and your passport must be valid for

at least 6 months from the date of entry. You will need a passport photo.

Officially, visas are not available on the Lao border. Many people have reported successfully obtaining visas here but don't rely on it. Travellers using the Lao border should try to arrange visa paperwork in advance in either Phnom Penh, Bangkok or Vientiane.

The **Cambodian Embassy in Bangkok**, 185 Rajdamri Rd, T+66-254 6630, issues visas in 1 day if you apply in the morning, as does the **Consulate General in HCMC**, Vietnam, 41 Phung Khac Khoan, T+84-8829 2751, and in **Hanoi** at 71 Tran Hung Dao St, T+84-4942 4788. In both Vietnam and Thailand, travel agencies are normally willing to obtain visas for a small fee. Cambodia has a few missions overseas from which visas can be obtained.

Note Travellers leaving by land must ensure that their Vietnam visa specifies Moc Bai or Chau Doc as points of entry otherwise they could be turned back. You can apply for a Cambodian visa in HCMC and collect in Hanoi and vice versa.

Visa extensions

Extensions can be obtained at the Department for Foreigners on the road to the airport, T023-581558 (passport photo required). Most travel agents arrange visa extensions for around US$40 for 30 days. Those overstaying their visas are fined US$5 per day; officials at land crossings often try to squeeze out more.

Weights and measures

Metric.

Index <small>*Entries in bold refer to maps or temple plans*</small>

FOOTPRINT

Features

Credits

Footprint credits

Editor: Nicola Gibbs, Felicity Laughton
Editorial assistant: Fernanda Dutra
Production and layout: Patrick Dawson
Maps: Kevin Feeney
Colour section: Angus Dawson

Publisher: Patrick Dawson
Managing Editor: Felicity Laughton
Administration: Elizabeth Taylor
Advertising sales and marketing:
John Sadler, Kirsty Holmes

Photography credits

Front cover: Vicnt / Dreamstime.com
Back cover: Simonhack / Dreamstime.
com; Secondshot / Dreamstime.com

Colour section

Inside front cover: kravka/shutterstock.
com, Pete Niesen/shutterstock.com.
Page 1: Luciano Mortula/shutterstock.
com. **Page 2**: SuperStock / Wolfgang
Kaehler. **Page 4**: weltreisender.tj/
shutterstock.com. **Page 5**: Waj/
shutterstock.com, Im Perfect Lazybones/
shutterstock.com. **Page 6**: Nestor
Noci/ shutterstock.com, Tonkin image/
shutterstock.com. **Page 8**: Narathorn/
shutterstock.com.

Printed in Spain by GraphyCems

The content of *Angkor 2nd edition* has
been taken directly from Footprint's
Cambodia Handbook 7th edition.

Publishing information

Footprint Handbooks Angkor
2nd edition
© Footprint Handbooks Ltd
April 2015

ISBN: 978 1 910120 22 4
CIP DATA: A catalogue record
for this book is available from
the British Library

® Footprint Handbooks and the
Footprint mark are a registered
trademark of Footprint Handbooks Ltd

Published by Footprint
6 Riverside Court
Lower Bristol Road
Bath BA2 3DZ, UK
T +44 (0)1225 469141
footprinttravelguides.com

Distributed in the USA by
National Book Network, Inc.

Every effort has been made to ensure
that the facts in this guidebook are
accurate. However, travellers should still
obtain advice from consulates, airlines,
etc about travel and visa requirements
before travelling. The authors and
publishers cannot accept responsibility
for any loss, injury or inconvenience
however caused.